Consolations of Insignificance

Consolations of Insignificance

A New Zealand Diplomatic Memoir

Terence O'Brien

TE HERENGA WAKA
UNIVERSITY PRESS
VICTORIA UNIVERSITY OF WELLINGTON

TE HERENGA WAKA UNIVERSITY PRESS
Te Herenga Waka – Victoria University of Wellington
PO Box 600 Wellington
teherengawakapress.co.nz

A catalogue record is available from
the National Library of New Zealand

ISBN 978-1-776-92139-3

Printed in Singapore by Markono Print Media Pte Ltd

CONTENTS

Preface   7

Foreword   11

1. Introduction   15

2. Asian Preludes   22

3. European Preoccupations   44

4. Near Abroad   62

5. Touching Base   77

6. Lakeside   83

7. Back to the Future   93

8. Homeland   112

9. On the East River   131

10. Absconding at Twilight   155

List of acronyms   171

Timeline   174

Index   175

PREFACE

This insightful book on Terence Christopher O'Brien's life's work is one that I recommend to all who want a better understanding of how New Zealand and the world developed their thinking over the past 60 years following the end of World War II.

That era also marked the beginning of a new age in science and the beginning of the revolution that remarkable developments in technology had ushered in. The end of World War II was hastened by the dropping of two nuclear bombs on Japan. The massive destruction caused by that decision focused the minds of leaders across subsequent generations that they didn't have unlimited rights to use all the power that science had placed in their hands.

Terence was fully aware of the fearful power now in the hands of his fellow humans and the need to control and manage that power. The world has established various structures to help minimise either accidental or, more frightening, deliberate use of nuclear weapons. The world is still a dangerous place and we continue to need the skills of diplomats like Terence O'Brien, who patiently bring together like-minded leaders to try and ensure that nuclear destruction never happens. New Zealand, with the commitment and advice of its senior diplomats, played a leading role in advancing the cause of nuclear disarmament. This work required considerable effort and commitment, and the courage to take and hold a different position than many of our long-term friends.

In many ways the book tells the story of how a small distant country set out to carve a unique and independent foreign policy, not only to express our view of how the world must move forward, but also to express our view on the need for nuclear disarmament. There is no rational reason in a world challenged regarding resources that vast sums are spent on developing nuclear weapons, especially since, when developed, they require extra billions to be spent to ensure they are stored in a manner that maintains their security.

New Zealand's move to adopting a more independent foreign and defence policy started to emerge in the Vietnam War era. A war fought in Asia helped New Zealand policy makers to shift their gaze from its normal focus on conflicts emerging from Western Europe.

This was the era when New Zealand transitioned from being a colony of the once all-powerful British Empire to being a proudly independent country that developed its own independent policies, including its 'nuclear free' policies. These were very controversial when introduced but are now seen as a defining development in New Zealand's history.

My experience in working with Terence over a wide range of policy issues was that he always knew the detailed history of the issue and therefore had a very constructive input in discussions. We first worked together when I was Minister of Labour (1978–84) and was elected President of the International Labor Organisation (ILO). The ILO back then had a bigger membership of nations than the UN. The conference lasted a month in Geneva and was a complex group drawn from a wide cross-section of society, with many different political structures, beliefs and agendas. Terence provided great assistance and advice over the month that the conference covered. It was for me also a period of great opportunities as I engaged at close quarters with senior political leaders from countries that many New Zealanders wouldn't be able to locate on a map.

Terence was again there to advise and help a few years later when as Prime Minister I was in New York to address the UN General Assembly and later to attend a function hosted by US President George H. W. Bush. Following the function, we had arranged that President Bush and myself would meet to help rebuild relations between our two countries following the breakdown caused by New Zealand's non-nuclear policy.

President Bush had a military general with him and I had Terence O'Brien, and the four of us had an open and honest discussion on the implications of New Zealand's non-nuclear policy on US–NZ relations. It was at that informal meeting that President Bush advised me that he was about to announce that the US was going to remove nuclear weapons from surface vessels. A big step forward.

Terence O'Brien's book covers a number of key events over the past 60 years and he brings to the story the insights of a trained professional who was closely involved in the events he comments on. The book is also a reminder of how New Zealand has dealt with big, internationally complex issues like nuclear disarmament. Terence has served New Zealand well by putting his recall of events on paper to encourage successor generations to continue to lead on big issues.

Jim Bolger
35th Prime Minister of New Zealand
October 2023

FOREWORD

Terence was not born in New Zealand but the foundations for his deep devotion to the country were laid early on. His father, Wing Commander Oliver James O'Brien (Paddy), was an RAF pilot and was posted to various air force bases in Britain in the lead up to World War II. He lived with his wife, Peggy, a concert pianist, and it was in Aylesbury, Buckinghamshire, that Terence was born on 6 January 1936, the first of their three children.

Their second child Bridget was born when Terence was four and a half years old, on the day that the Germans invaded the Low Countries (10 May 1940), and Terence vaguely remembered this event – one of his earliest memories. In the same year, Paddy was posted to Mount Maunganui in New Zealand to train RNZAF pilots. Peggy, Terence and Bridget followed soon after, arriving in May 1941 on board the dilapidated, slow SS *Perseus*, a coal-burning merchant ship – fortunately avoiding almost certain death on the SS *Napier Star*, on which they had tried to travel and which was torpedoed by a German U-boat and sunk with almost total loss of life. The family stayed at Mount Maunganui for about a year and a half. Here Terence began his life as a New Zealander, walking to school on sand in bare feet.

Paddy was then sent to the air force base at Wigram. The family lived in Christchurch with Terence attending school there until 1944, after which they were once more relocated – this time to Wellington where sister Jane was born. Terence would recount a vivid memory of jubilant crowds and tremendous celebrations in Wellington on VE Day, 1945. In 1946, aged ten, Terence sailed with his family back to Britain, where he would spend his secondary school years being taught by the Jesuits at Beaumont College.

Paddy's appointment in 1950 first as Deputy and later as New Zealand's Chief Inspector of Air Accidents saw the rest of the O'Brien family return to Wellington, with Terence joining them in 1954. He completed a stint at Victoria University and worked in the summer holidays shifting wool bales on the wharves. Terence then travelled back to Britain to read history at University College, Oxford, only to return to New Zealand in 1958, joining the then Department of External Affairs the following year aged 23.

In these early years it could be said that Terence completed his apprenticeship to becoming a New Zealander, at the same time experiencing the itinerant lifestyle which he was to lead as a diplomat. Apart from a posting to London in the late 1960s, Terence never lived in Britain again. He became a naturalised New Zealand citizen in 1962, at the age of 26, eventually voluntarily surrendering his UK passport and renouncing British citizenship. His first overseas posting as a New Zealand diplomat was to Bangkok in 1963, where shortly afterwards he married Elizabeth (née Elworthy). They would go on to have four children, John (born 1969), Georgia (born 1972), Daniel (born 1975) and Timothy (born 1976). For 35 years Terence would faithfully serve New Zealand, including postings as the country's representative in Brussels, Geneva and New York. His significant contribution to New Zealand's discourse on foreign policy continued through his subsequent work as Founding Director of the Centre for Strategic Studies at Te Herenga Waka – Victoria University of Wellington, and, following retirement in 2000, through his commentary, writing and public speaking.

For Terence's 80th birthday, his family established a scholarship to honour his longstanding professional commitment to international relations and strategic studies, and help equip students with a career interest in professional diplomacy. He retained a keen interest in New Zealand's international relations until his death in Wellington on 30 December 2022, aged 86.

Terence fell on his feet when he became a diplomat. It suited his talents and interests perfectly. He was a voracious reader with elephant-like recall not only for what he read but also for people and places. He enjoyed nothing more than a robust discussion on current affairs and was particularly interested in listening to and learning from the opinions of younger generations, a fervent believer in keeping an open mind. He loved travel, enjoying the deeper understanding of cultures and people that it brought. As former New Zealand Prime Minister Helen Clark remarked 'He was always prepared to offer free and frank advice, and was well respected for his integrity and expertise.' Among the tributes received by his family at the time of his death, colleagues spoke of the generosity he showed taking time to mentor them in their junior years, his willingness to share his knowledge and expertise and the humour and warmth he injected into proceedings. He never lost his joie-de-vivre.

Terence's career brought with it a varied and colourful life which we are blessed to have shared with him. We are happy that he was able to record some of the high- (and low-) lights of his time doing what he loved, representing New Zealand as an independent voice on the global stage.

Elizabeth and children,
John, Georgia, Daniel and Timothy

1. INTRODUCTION

When measuring human existence, the timespan of one generation is reckoned at 30 years. This tale of involvement with the international affairs of New Zealand, beginning in 1959 with my entry into what was then known as the Department of External Affairs, harks back over two generations. The reminiscences are, almost by definition, choosy. They represent mementos, sometimes half recollected, of experience.

A wise person once remarked that each generation imagines itself to be more intelligent than the one that went before it, and wiser than the one that comes after it. As far as diplomatic experience is concerned, it is a fact of life that the various situations that one successively occupies have been inhabited by others, both before and afterwards, and often with far greater distinction. It is part of human nature too that individual versions of, and verdicts about, events differ between those who encounter the same or similar experience. That certainly applies to this chronicle.

The speed of modern change confuses memory. One difficulty looking back over two generations is moreover to distinguish between what one thought at the time, and what one thinks today. A life of recurrent international commuting also means periodic separation from where the real action is domestically, although real action internationally occurs readily on the doorstep of New Zealand's external presence. Diplomacy is an extended apprenticeship – of 'learning on the job'. Interspersed with a cavalcade of work in foreign places, work at home base in Wellington, in different capacities and for differing lengths of time, helped to keep my feet on, or nearer, the ground. The longest slice of consecutive time I spent personally in Wellington in MFAT work was four years. Twenty out of 34 years were spent overseas, followed by a final six at Victoria University in Wellington.

What is certain is that diplomatic life is a nomadic existence that tests personal and family wellbeing – in our family of four children, only one was born in New Zealand. The danger of disconnection from homeland life experience is an occupational hazard. This tale includes the pre-digital era, before the existence of computers, email, Facebook, Google, Twitter, Skype or Zoom, and in advance of such inventions as cell phones, faxes or shredders. In those times New Zealand diplomatic experience overseas was definitely a more remote existence. Embassies were not subject to close oversight, second guessing from head office, or scrutiny by media, as those in today's world are.

On top of all that there was scepticism, during the earlier years within New Zealand, about whether the country actually needed diplomats. Their existence was viewed as an extravagance for a small country whose trading and economic interests were surely and sufficiently served by nimble, resourceful entrepreneurs and, if necessary, ex-politicians resurrected as senior diplomatic envoys. Even as greater professionalism was gradually achieved, cheeseparing budgets under successive New Zealand governments reflected such preconceptions. Indeed it was not until the present century began that the purse strings for the conduct of those New Zealand relations were materially loosened under Foreign Minister Winston Peters.

Over two generations, New Zealand experience internationally increasingly confirmed that diversifying New Zealand's trade and economic opportunities depended squarely upon durable political connexions designed to reinforce trust; and that face-to-face dealings through a resident diplomatic presence in foreign capitals directly served that interest. In a broader sense there was recognition too that New Zealand's very warrant to be a successful global trader rested upon a solid contribution, within its means, to the cause of international peace and good order. A small, professional, fully trained and equipped New Zealand defence force was a national asset.

Over the same two generations the administration in Wellington of New Zealand's external interests wore a succession of hats – the Department of External Affairs (1943) became the Ministry of Foreign Affairs (1969), then the Ministry of External Relations and Trade (1988), then the Ministry of Foreign Affairs and Trade (1993). This successive transfiguration reflected that New Zealand's foreign policy and trade policy (as distinct from the business of trade promotion) are inextricably connected, and that professionalisation of a government operation to reflect that reality was required. The Ministry's officials had many turf battles with the Department of Trade and Industry over providing trade policy advice to ministers; this needless competition was a waste of time and effort, as I discovered from personal experience.

◌ෛ

Before digging into the undergrowth, it may be useful to slice and dice the first-hand experiences chronicled here into five different (although related) contexts. First is the context of *Asia* with a posting in Bangkok, followed by subsequent aid policy dealings in capitals across the region, involvement with establishment of New Zealand's physical presence in China, and subsequently extensive exposure to Asian thinking about how best to nourish habits of cooperation (politically, economically, commercially and for security) to reflect Asia's modern transformation and accomplishments.

A second context was involvement with the consequences for New Zealand of Britain's entry into *Europe* in the late 1960s, early 1970s and 1980s, involving two postings in Brussels, a stint in London, and assignment in Geneva. In this time of Brexit, New Zealand's obsessive concern of nearly two generations ago about enlargement of the European Community is demonstrably yesterday's story. Is it indeed relevant at all? Yet the experience administered undeniable shock to New Zealand's sense of place in the world, and over the generation that followed it compelled diversification of trade opportunities and therefore of foreign relations. It appreciably widened the horizons and the interests of the country.

The *South Pacific* provided a third context, with an assignment in Rarotonga, leadership of various aid missions throughout the region and later oversight in Wellington of New Zealand Pacific policy inside MFAT, as an Assistant Secretary. That last responsibility included involvement in a six-month prime ministerial-mandated review of New Zealand–South Pacific policies, involving government, non-government and business interests. Wide-ranging consultation included every member country in the South Pacific Forum, plus French territories, and occurred at the very time when a spate of political disorder was marking New Zealand's

Pacific neighbourhood. Nothing quite as extensive had been tried before. If the South Pacific had ever enjoyed 'an age of innocence' it would be true to say that this was indeed conclusively ending by the 1980s–1990s.

The *New Zealand non-nuclear policy* provided a fourth context in offshore assignment in Brussels (the home of NATO, the North Atlantic Treaty Organisation), and onshore responsibility later as Assistant Secretary for oversight of New Zealand's political, security and economic relationship with Australia, which had severely rebuked the New Zealand non-nuclear decision. The 1951 Australia–New Zealand–United States (ANZUS) military alliance was rendered inoperable by the United States as far as New Zealand was concerned. The review of New Zealand's post-ANZUS relationship with Australia became critical, as did, of course, build back of a (changed) relationship with Washington. A sense that New Zealand had 'lost its way' because of the non-nuclear policy was not one that I personally shared. Some colleagues, whose judgements I otherwise respected, nonetheless felt that loss strongly. As MFAT's own online account of that period admits, the policy caused 'long faces' amongst officials at the time.

A fifth and final context was involvement with *multilateral diplomacy* in Bangkok, Geneva and New York. It covered the whole gamut from trade to security, and much in between. Bilateral diplomacy – country-to-country dealings – is all about relationship building over the long haul to protect and promote New Zealand's national interests. Multilateral diplomacy involves working with like-minded countries in international institutions to set rules that govern or guard standards of collective international behaviour. The business of forming coalitions of interest and encouraging collective action in those international institutions benefits from cumulative frontline exposure to the particular chemistry of multilateral diplomacy. Involvement with obtaining a sternly contested New Zealand seat on the 1993–94 United Nations Security Council, after a long New Zealand absence, provided a case in point.

☙

In 1959 External Affairs, as it was then known, was approaching the end of its adolescent years. It consisted of a small cast headed by Alister McIntosh and other revered founding fathers, housed in a dozen or so rooms adjacent to the Prime Minister's office on the top floor of Parliament Buildings, supporting a small New Zealand presence overseas of ten diplomatic posts.

It was largely a masculine preserve in Wellington. Although there was a female stenographic pool, where manuscripts for typing had to be deposited and collected, there were very few women amongst the External Affairs staff. There was an expectation, if not a rule, that those women who chose to marry would resign, since they were considered unsuitable for posting abroad. Spouses of officers serving abroad, moreover, could only obtain employment in the country of their husband's posting with the permission of the resident New Zealand Ambassador or High Commissioner. Patriarchy ruled.

Co-location of premises in Parliament provided curiosities. Even the most junior newcomer soon experienced riding up and down in the parliamentary elevator in the sole company of the Prime Minister. External Affairs staff were also extended access to Bellamys, the parliamentary bar, which was housed in the former Government House, a wooden building built in 1871 where the New Zealand Parliament's Beehive now stands. The ramshackle premises had suffered prolonged neglect.

In the days of six o'clock closing of pubs throughout New Zealand, but not in Parliament, Bellamys access provided in principle an enticement, except that it was a totally forlorn experience. A small windowless space with a brown lino floor, light brown walls and hand-me-down high stools constituted the Messengers Bar, where External Affairs staff enjoyed the 'privilege' of after-hours refreshment. Barmen flourishing long hoses filled jugs and four-ounce beer glasses. Bar food was available, but it had first passed through the three separate accompanying bars for MPs, for friends and for media, so by the time the food arrived on the counter at the lowly Messengers Bar, it had been fingered, sampled, or even gnawed higher up the line. Pigs' trotters were a speciality of the house.

There were additional benefits. One could purchase a bottle of specially blended Bellamys whisky. More bizarrely, tins of toheroa soup were also sold over the bar. Toheroa was a highly protected shellfish, and harvesting was banned just a few years later. Purchase of the protected delicacy was deemed a privilege for elected parliamentarians – a case perhaps of one protected species enjoying the privilege of devouring another?

CR

I had returned to New Zealand in 1959 after three years at Oxford University studying modern history, and was lodging with my parents in Lower Hutt. My father was Chief Inspector of Air Accidents. This was an active and intrusive responsibility, as flying accidents in New Zealand, at least in those times, occurred predominantly at weekends, thereby interrupting my father's leisure time. The job required hurried emergency visits to crash sites up and down the country, and the retrieval of key damaged aircraft parts which had first to be brought home for safekeeping, because official storage was, just like New Zealand itself, closed over weekends. Our garage and hallway were frequently littered with mangled pieces of wrecked aircraft metal. I had approached the New Zealand High Commission in London about job prospects and they advised me to contact the Department of External Affairs upon my return to New Zealand.

My introduction into the Department was a prosaic, down-to-earth, slightly cock-eyed experience. There was no dedicated induction course. A newcomer was rotated through different sections of the small department, relying upon different heads of those sections for guidance and education. Some mentors were good, some not so good.

Part of my ordainment involved an early one-year secondment outside the Department, to the External Assessments Bureau (EAB), housed adjacent to the British High Commission in the Government Insurance Building on Jervois Quay, Wellington, opposite the Queens Wharf Entrance. I never quite understood the reasons behind that particular EAB co-location. My responsibilities included updating and extending a 'current intelligence guide', which was a New Zealand fact-book on countries of Asia. One notable task was preparing potted biographies along with other basic material for Prime Minister Walter Nash's 1960 visit to Moscow, which was a first for New Zealand. But overall there was scant benefit from the secondment in terms of understanding the methods, the chemistry and the demands of the Department of External Affairs.

The expectation (but not the rule) was that after three years, more or less, of this baptism the newly minted officer would be posted to one of the small number of New Zealand diplomatic missions. The brighter recruits moved through the hoops purposefully – in my case I toiled more than three years before being posted away to Bangkok.

2. ASIAN PRELUDES

Elizabeth and I first met in 1961. She was living in Christchurch. Early encounters were spasmodic but our decision to marry was taken just as affirmation of my first posting to Thailand came through. We decided then to marry in Bangkok. When I departed, Elizabeth remained to complete her Canterbury University degree, and one of my first tasks upon arrival in Bangkok was therefore to plan practical details for an event of which I had no experience, and in a place which was uncharted territory. The New Zealand Ambassador Sir Stephen Weir knew Elizabeth's parents and he kindly offered his residence for the wedding reception. The ceremony itself was duly held in 1963 at the American Catholic missionary church Wat Mahatai, built in the style of a Thai Buddhist temple. We had unwittingly planned a date slap in the middle of the monsoon season. The thunderous downpour of continuous torrential rain on the verandah roof of Sir Stephen's residence during the wedding reception drowned all conversation, and (happily) rendered speech-making immaterial.

The image as I arrived in late 1962 of the New Zealand Embassy to Thailand, housed in a pleasant two-storey converted Bangkok private home with a large balcony and garden, remains clear. It was situated down a short lane just off one of Bangkok's main thoroughfares – the tree-lined Sathorn Road with its accompanying canal (klong). Canals were still abundant and earned Bangkok (at least amongst Europeans) the title 'the Venice of the East'. The Embassy setting has long since been obliterated as Bangkok has modernised. Due to its location, both the lane and the grounds were prone to flooding in the monsoon season, obliging staff members to paddle barefoot to and from the entrance to their transport.

It took about 20 minutes to walk to the Embassy via a footbridge over the Sathorn klong, from the small two-bedroom house in a dead-end lane that Elizabeth and I rented. Walking was feasible in the relatively cool early morning, but at midday and in the early evening, the Bangkok heat was a strong disincentive. Indeed heat and humidity dominated our existence. The rented house had no kitchen, but in the back garden stood a shed with an earthen floor and charcoal stove where, in blast furnace conditions, food was prepared. That was an insurmountable test for any foreign newlyweds. Elizabeth and I were obliged to employ a cheerful smiling cook, Charoen, who became vital to our existence.

These were the days before the massive shopping malls cooled by intensive air conditioning which now characterise the cities of modern Southeast Asia. At that time, moreover, the holy grail for official New Zealand living in foreign parts, the Overseas Handbook (OSH), allowed for just one domestic air conditioner per occupied bedroom. We were therefore permitted to install one which provided, in theory, cool space upstairs in our small house. We quickly discovered that when operating it regularly blew the fuses on all the lights plus the fridge, as well as the lights in our Thai neighbours' houses. We then realised they had surreptitiously connected their lighting to our house grid to save on overheads. Downstairs the house had attractive polished teak floors but no windows or walls, just wooden slatted doors opening to a patio, all designed for catching the Bangkok breeze that flowed gently but erratically.

The OSH likewise prescribed that as far as office transport was concerned, only the Ambassador's car could be air-conditioned. Other staff were obliged to travel on official business, perspiring copiously in Embassy transport, through dense Bangkok traffic. There were air conditioners in the working spaces at the Embassy itself, but they were large, noisy, window-rattling contraptions, prone to breakdown.

I arrived at the Embassy towards the end of 1962 to occupy the bottom-most rung on its diplomatic ladder – Third Secretary. I had responsibility for oversight of the New Zealand aid programme in Thailand – and also in Vietnam, where New Zealand had no resident presence – but more of that later. I had had no real background in aid work during my initiation in Wellington. New Zealand was a small aid donor and there appeared to be a blithe assumption at head office that such work could readily be handled by junior and mid-level diplomatic officers without much knowledge or practical experience.

No formal language training had been offered, and there were no fluent Thai speakers amongst the Bangkok diplomatic staff. Some of us acquired a level of 'kitchen Thai' required for shopping and the like, but nothing beyond. That was an obvious handicap for an aid officer whose responsibilities necessitated frequent travel beyond the capital, particularly to northeast Thailand, which Wellington had designated a special focus for New Zealand aid, and where spoken English was rare. The flagship New Zealand project was the design, construction and equipping of an agricultural faculty for a new university at Khon Kaen that required regular on-site liaison and inspection.

This was well before such places as the World Bank or Organisation for Economic Development (OECD) had turned their attention to devising principles and practices to guide aid donor and recipient relationships and policies. Although New Zealand had a handful of Volunteer Service Abroad workers on the ground in Thailand, non-governmental organisations (NGOs) and private philanthropy had not yet really entered the field of overseas development assistance (ODA) and emergency response either. That was to materially change over the decades ahead.

∞

I was also New Zealand liaison representative to the United Nations regional office in Bangkok – the Economic Commission for Asia and the Far East (ECAFE, now known as ESCAP: Economic and Social Commission for Asia and the Pacific) – charged with encouraging regional cooperation in economic and social development. It provided an introduction to collective multilateral diplomacy that came to preoccupy important parts of my later apprenticeship. The work included Embassy support for senior public servants sent from Wellington to attend multiple workshops, seminars and meetings on trade, industry, business, export and import policy, and the like.

Annual ministerial conferences in successive capitals attracted senior political figures to represent New Zealand, like Deputy Prime Minister John Marshall and Deputy Secretary Foss Shanahan, an External Affairs founding father who was a legend in his own time. At the 1964 ministerial conference in Teheran, Shanahan took over delegation leadership after Marshall suffered a heart attack which forced him into a six-week recuperation in the Iranian capital, even as other delegation members, including myself, departed. It would be wrong to overestimate ECAFE accomplishments, but given the limited extent of official New Zealand connexions throughout Asia at the time, participation in the only established regional economic forum served to compensate for an otherwise sparse presence.

Multitasking at the Bangkok Embassy was the norm. As shredders had not yet been invented, the junior diplomatic staff were rostered each fortnight to destroy the Embassy's secret and confidential papers that were no longer needed. The Embassy was responsible for New Zealand representation at the headquarters of the Southeast Asia Treaty Organisation (SEATO), which emitted screeds of classified military plans and papers. Thus there was a fair amount of material requiring regular disposal – in a large, rusty 44-gallon drum in the Embassy's back garden.

Disposal was exquisitely hot work in the Bangkok sun. But the larger challenge was the fact that the New Zealand Embassy's back garden fence was all that physically separated our premises from the very large Soviet Embassy next door. The East–West Cold War and containment of communism were the absolute fixation at that time (witnessed particularly by the deteriorating situation in neighbouring Vietnam). Special care was needed to prevent burning papers or charred fragments of documents marked TOP SECRET or CONFIDENTIAL from floating out of the 44-gallon drum in the gentle Bangkok breeze, over the fence and into communist premises. There were occasions when even the most energetic chasing and arm waving failed to halt a leaking of charred confidences.

At the time the Bangkok Embassy was one of five missions that New Zealand operated in Asia. It was, along with the Tokyo Embassy, the only one outside Wellington's preferred selection of English-speaking capitals (Singapore, Hong Kong and Kuala Lumpur), although Jakarta was soon to be opened. Official New Zealand understanding of East Asia at the time was clearly influenced by an Anglocentric perspective, embellished by American perceptions, especially as conflict in Vietnam deepened.

A principal reason for the Embassy was that Bangkok provided the headquarters for SEATO, of which New Zealand had become a founding member in 1954. Only two out of its eight members, Thailand and the Philippines, were actually from Southeast Asia; the remainder were US military allies. SEATO was a paper castle. It did not involve joint command of any standing military force, although New Zealand supplied a small logistics detachment of Royal New Zealand Air Force (RNZAF) Bristol Freighters, based at Khorat in northeast Thailand.

The council of member state representatives met regularly at ambassadorial level. The New Zealand Ambassador, Sir Stephen Weir, was our representative. He was a notable New Zealand soldier, having served as artillery commander with the New Zealand Division in Greece, North Africa and Italy during World War II. Later in Italy he transferred out of the New Zealand force to become the only non-British officer in World War II to command a British division.

Sir Stephen's qualifications were sterling, and not just with respect to SEATO. Despite a legendary veneration for monarchy, Thailand was at that time governed by a dictatorship of senior military men with a firm grip on the levers of power. Their collective firsthand experience of real fighting was negligible, however, so they had a certain professional respect for people with authentic warfare experience. Sir Stephen's credentials were exemplary, and his access to top government circles (always a preoccupation for ambassadors) was pretty well unmatched. He enjoyed almost weekly golf at the Bangkok Sports Club with the Thai Prime Minister, an army general. Other foreign envoys were not so fortunate.

Sir Stephen had a commanding presence and a voice accustomed to authority. In his person and voice he embodied everyone's idea of a 'modern major general' sent from central casting. He was a conservative thinker, but he was fair minded and listened attentively even to junior embassy staff views. It was natural that he took close interest in the unfolding Vietnam War, and his office wall sported a floor-to-ceiling map of the whole area. Armed with a long pointer in the presence of visitors, his briefings looked and sounded the complete part.

A visit to Thailand by Prime Minister Keith Holyoake in 1964 (the first ever by a New Zealand leader) was the signature diplomatic event during my time. He was on a tour of Indonesia, Malaya and Thailand. He came with his wife and delegation, including the Secretary of External Affairs, Alister McIntosh, as an official guest of the Thai Government. Thailand's reputation for hospitality is justly famous. Junior embassy staff were not much involved in the high-level dealings that marked the visit, but we were included in the socialising. My own involvement taught one early lesson for the novice: care must always be taken in diplomacy whenever humour is introduced into situations where there is not shared language or culture.

The sumptuous dinner offered by the Thai Prime Minister for Mr Holyoake in one of Bangkok's major palaces proved a case in point. It was a masterpiece of decoration and style involving an enormous horseshoe table, around which sat Thai politicians, aristocracy and military, with light from glittering chandeliers reflecting on the beautiful Thai silk dresses of the women and the white dinner jackets and copious military decorations of the men. As befitted my very modest status, I was parked at the furthest end of the horseshoe table alongside the kitchen entrance, where squads of serving staff passed continuously by. My table companions were, on one side, an army colonel who revealed himself to be the Thai PM's food taster, which involved several quick forays into the kitchen during proceedings to ensure no poisons in the fare; and on the other, Mike Nicolaidi, the New Zealand Press Association (NZPA) journalist travelling with the Holyoake party.

Our Prime Minister had been made familiar with the fact that in Tolstoy's novel *War and Peace*, a certain Count Nicolai features amongst the characters. As a consequence he had coined a nickname for Mike Nicolaidi of 'the Count'. It was a typical in-joke amongst the travelling New Zealand party. When the moment arrived at the glittering dinner for official speeches, Holyoake rose, thanking the Thai hosts for their spectacular hospitality and remarking in his famously sonorous tones how he and his wife, coming as they did from a small remote country, were particularly honoured by the gathering of high-ranking Thai princes and princesses who had assembled to greet his party. That did not mean, he boomed, New Zealand was itself totally devoid of people with aristocratic rank; indeed one such was travelling in his party – and with a pause for dramatic effect and a sweep of the arm, he gestured towards the far reaches of the horseshoe table and intoned 'I refer of course to Count Nicolaidi'.

Poor Mike was covered in embarrassment. There were half-suppressed guffaws from some New Zealanders but an impressive wall of absolute polite silence from the the glittering multitude of Thai dignitaries, and most especially from the Chief of Thai Protocol. On the face of it a gross breach of etiquette had been committed by seating such a distinguished visitor alongside the kitchen and the taster. Holyoake seemed to sense then that something was not now quite right with the chemistry of his audience, and the remainder of his address subsided rapidly like air from a punctured balloon.

Other pitfalls intruded. New Zealand had committed in Thailand to aid support for economic and social development along the Mekong River bordering Laos and Cambodia, a project coordinated through the United Nations. New Zealand had gifted three or four newly invented Hamilton jet boats to the project. This was amongst the very earliest examples of leveraging government aid resources to display New Zealand manufacturing capacity (and thereby enhance commercial possibilities) while at the same time meeting authentic needs. In Thailand the effectiveness of this dual purpose stratagem was initially uncertain, however, because at the Embassy we had encountered much difficulty in keeping tabs on just how useful the new jet boats were proving on the Mekong. Our Thai colleagues were notably elusive on the matter.

In 1964 a TVNZ team visited to make a documentary on New Zealand aid and other policies in Southeast Asia. They wanted to visit the Mekong Valley before crossing over into Laos, and the Embassy offered its Land Rover plus my services to assist the expedition. TVNZ gratefully accepted. Over a period of days and nights we travelled the long course of the river, filming and interviewing, but our enquiries as to the whereabouts of the New Zealand jet boats drew a blank in more than one place.

Finally we arrived at the riverside town of Nong Khai, from where we were to cross over by barge to Laos (nowadays there is a handsome Australian-built bridge). I accompanied the four-man team on a stroll along the riverbank one evening after a meal. At a certain point we sighted a group of weed-infested boats rusting in the shallows of the Mekong. One of the journalists curiously scraped rubbish away from the hull of one of the desolate boats, and revealed, prettily etched on a plaque, 'a gift from the people of New Zealand to the people of Thailand' or words to that effect. We had found the jet boats!

Excitedly the journalists rushed back to the hotel for cameras and lighting. They took a lingering close-up shot of the cleaned up plaque, allowing the camera then to pan slowly backwards and capture on wide angle the forlorn dilapidated trio of disused boats. The producer gleefully pronounced himself well satisfied, and insisted the take would provide an admirable opening shot for the entire documentary.

Needless to say, as the aid officer, the most junior on the embassy staff, I became decidedly nervous about all of this. Would I be held responsible for carelessly discrediting New Zealand's aid performance and manufacturing prowess? Upon return a few days later to Bangkok I hurriedly sought out the Ambassador to explain the whole episode. He agreed we should alert Wellington forthwith to possible surprises in the TVNZ finished product. In the event I never actually saw the documentary, and the jet boat operational faults, I learnt, were remedied.

◌

The challenges of aid work in Thailand were superseded by the complexities of parallel work in Vietnam, which was added to my portfolio. In the early 1960s New Zealand had no resident official presence on the ground in the South Vietnamese capital of Saigon (today, Ho Chi Minh City). In 1962, following persuasion from the United States to contribute to prevention of a deteriorating Vietnamese humanitarian situation, New Zealand had agreed to support an American-led medical aid programme with a five- to six-person civilian surgical team. The place of work chosen was the Binh Dinh provincial capital of Quy Nhon, situated on the coast some hundreds of kilometres north of Saigon. Even though outright conflict had not yet broken out, the security situation in Binh Dinh was unsettling – Viet Cong insurgents held ground some 15 kilometres from the town.

This was a brave undertaking given the rising levels of insurgency and the absence of a permanent New Zealand diplomatic presence on the ground in Saigon. The project exceeded by a considerable margin anything previously in New Zealand aid experience. Wellington had decided that the Bangkok Embassy should assume oversight responsibility and the Ambassador was to be duly accredited to South Vietnam – but no physical presence would be established in the South Vietnamese capital. Even without the benefit of hindsight and in the best of all worlds, this commitment appeared hazardous. A matter of just weeks after my arrival in Thailand, I was despatched on the first of multiple visits to Saigon that divided my attention for the next year and a half between Thailand and Vietnam.

Among those several visits, I accompanied Sir Stephen Weir to Saigon to present his credentials in 1963, as New Zealand's first (non-resident) envoy to Vietnam. There were eccentric moments. Sir Stephen had decided that he should take his own transport as an economy measure (the hire of large official cars in Saigon was costly – and Wellington was demanding economies in the Embassy budget). He determined this could be done by enlisting use of a Bristol Freighter from the RNZAF detachment stationed at Khorat, where Sir Stephen's rank, reputation and authority carried weight. A Bristol Freighter was readily volunteered.

It flew down to Bangkok to pick up the party, consisting of Sir Stephen and Lady Weir, his driver and myself. At the airport we quickly discovered a problem. The official car, a Mercedes Benz, could be accommodated in the aircraft, but it was a very tight fit and once inside it was impossible to open the car doors. Sir Stephen promptly decided that he and Lady Weir should travel to Saigon inside the Mercedes sitting in the back seat, and the driver, who had of course no experience of Saigon topography, seated behind the wheel, with the New Zealand pennant displayed upon the bonnet. I was installed on the flight deck above the gloomy cargo space.

The Freighter lumbered noisily down to Saigon. We landed at Tan Son Nhut Air Base amidst a vast assembly of sleek F-105 US fighters, clusters of attack helicopters and the dark painted US Air Force heavy lift aircraft. The very sight of the squat-bellied Freighter was, as I could see through a flight deck window, attracting attention from American military ground staff who were clicking away with their cameras as we taxied into the parking area. But the best bit was still to to come: as the bulbous nose doors of the Freighter were opened, the shiny ambassadorial Mercedes appeared, moving sedately down the ramp with flag flying. The assembled Vietnamese protocol detachment was visibly impressed, and the growing crowd of American onlookers went into overdrive with their cameras. All that was lacking was a blare of trumpets and a choir.

Sir Stephen returned to Bangkok by the same means some four days later. I had accompanied him at the ceremonials involved with formal ambassadorial accreditation, which included a handshake with the ill-fated Vietnamese President Ngo Dinh Diem, who was soon to be assassinated in a military coup. I remained in Saigon, however, to try to advance the establishment of the surgical team project. Other governments solicited by the US for help with the surgical programme had all declined. New Zealand hoped the commitment might perhaps allow us to sidestep further American requests for direct military support in the deteriorating security situation. In the event, those hopes proved forlorn. Further US persuasion led to the commitment of New Zealand military engineers during my time there, and of combat troops after my posting ended.

The surgical team project ran into difficulties before it ever commenced substantive work. Members of the team, hastily despatched from New Zealand, were marooned in Saigon hotels for weeks because there was no team accommodation ready in Quy Nhon. That was the responsibility of the Vietnamese Government to provide. Moreover, the hospital itself remained dilapidated and without promised US medical equipment.

We had made other rods for our own back. The Department of External Affairs had assumed the task of selecting the individual team members, rather than choosing a leader and then allowing him or her to pick available colleagues. The inordinate delays, differing personalities, culture shock and general anxiety over the deteriorating security situation combined to produce tricky chemistry on the ground. It was touch and go as to whether there would be defections before the team had even begun their work. We had one of the more difficult team members removed from Quy Nhon (because of personality clashes) to another health project among the Montagnard tribes in the hill region at Da Lat. He finally exhausted Wellington's patience altogether, and I was instructed to convey a red card to him (in the form of a letter from Prime Minister Holyoake).

I was embroiled in trying to ensure the Vietnamese fulfilled their reponsibilities, liaising with the US aid authorities (who were in overall charge of America's countrywide surgical project and encountering difficulties on their own account) and trying to placate the New Zealand team's understandable dissatisfactions. The team leader, Michael Shackleton from Dunedin, with his wife Annabelle and their small children in tow, performed heroically, but grew profoundly irritated by perceptions of administrative shortcomings in Wellington and at the New Zealand Embassy in Bangkok. Nonetheless, Shackleton's insistence that the surgical unit treat all Vietnamese patients irrespective of who they were, including wounded Viet Cong insurgents, commanded respect, even while the disconcerted Vietnamese head of the hospital insisted upon handcuffing Viet Cong patients to their beds, much to the chagrin of the New Zealand nurses.

The online New Zealand government history of the country's Vietnam involvement remarks tersely that the surgical team faced 'staunch resistance from Vietnamese counterparts, inadequate facilities, and little practical support from New Zealand bureaucrats.' Michael Shackleton's own very readable account of the Quy Nhon experience (*Operation Vietnam*, published by Otago University Press) conveys the extent of the difficulties, and the depth of feeling which they incited. From the outset I implored New Zealand officials who occasionally visited from Wellington that a permanent resident New Zealand presence on the ground in Saigon was indispensable. The accredited Ambassador installed in distant Bangkok of course concurred.

At the end of 1963 the Shackleton team's assignment terminated. They had worked for just seven months at Quy Nhon but had laid essential foundations. They were replaced by a team with a new leader, Cam Maclaurin. The project endured under successive leaders until 1975, when New Zealand withdrew the civilian team and closed down the resident embassy as Saigon fell to the advancing Viet Cong and Viet Minh. Despite all the travail and decidedly inauspicious beginnings, the civilian medical personnel earned New Zealand a constructive reputation inside Vietnam that endured.

As the Maclaurin team arrived, a long-delayed decision was taken by Wellington to provide a permanent New Zealand presence on the ground in South Vietnam, with the arrival in Saigon in February 1964 of Natalie England, from the New Zealand Embassy in Paris, to be resident Charge d'Affaires. She set up shop in the Hotel Caravelle, the one modern high-rise building in downtown Saigon, owned by Air France. Up until this point facilities had been made available at the British Embassy, which lent practical support with typing and message sending to Wellington and Bangkok. The British were helpful, but with the passage of time the connection grew awkward, as the British themselves had firmly declined involvement in the US-led surgical team project and, more importantly, resisted any formal military commitment to halt the mounting insurgency, while later that year New Zealand reluctantly agreed to contribute military assistance, firstly in the form of army engineers.

The new arrangement finally relieved me of Vietnam responsibilities – or so I thought. In August 1964, barely five months after her arrival, Natalie England became the victim of a Viet Cong bomb attack on the Hotel Caravelle. The device exploded on the floor directly above the New Zealand premises about midday, when Natalie had just quit the office for lunch and was awaiting the lift outside. Had she been at her desk, she would certainly have been killed; as it was, she was injured by flying glass and debris and had to be invalided to Bangkok. The office was in smithereens.

Once more I was despatched to liaise with security officials (principally American and British) investigating the incident, with New Zealand army engineers now on the ground in Vietnam, and with the Vietnamese authorities, and to seek alternative premises. In a belief that lightning should not strike twice in the same place, it was accepted by Wellington that I should seek alternative office space in the Hotel Caravelle, which I did. Natalie's permanent replacement, Arthur Pope, subsequently moved the office to a building near the US Embassy.

In the present age of radicalised violence and terrorist threats, when security precautions are paramount for overseas New Zealand missions and staff, the 1964 Caravelle bombing hardly registers in official New Zealand foreign policy memory, although Ian McGibbon portrays it in his history *New Zealand's Vietnam War*. Natalie England quit the External Affairs Department not long afterwards. Her ordeal was finally recognised with inclusion in the honours list, but not until 2003.

Two possible motives for the bombing were suggested. One was that the Viet Cong wanted to demonstrate they had the ability to carry out a daylight attack upon a landmark building in downtown Saigon. A second explanation was that it was intended as a message to New Zealand, which had recently despatched the army engineers as a military contribution to a deteriorating security situation. In a discussion after my return in early 1965 with the Secretary of External Affairs in Wellington, Alister McIntosh, his sense was that there was indeed something in the second explanation. He had access to much more authoritative information than a mere apprentice like me, of course.

In 1963 the war had grown increasingly unpopular amongst the Vietnamese people in the South. Government troops and police had used live ammunition to suppress uprisings. My intermittent presence variously coincided with self-immolation by Buddhist monks in opposition to President Diem and his avaricious sister, periodic attempted military coups, Viet Cong bombing of Saigon cinemas, and the Vietnamese President's own assassination just weeks after the 1963 murder of John F. Kennedy in the United States. The inexorable build up of the US military presence accelerated quickly and was a pervasive backdrop to our aid work. By the end of 1964 there were 15,000 US troops in the country; by the end of 1965 that had risen to nearly 200,000 troops, and that number more than doubled in ensuing years.

A well informed but sceptical Saigon foreign press corps came to exert much influence in Washington. Amongst them were two Kiwis: Nick Turner, who was the Reuters correspondent and a shrewd judicious newsman, and Peter Arnett, who much later became a lion amongst CNN reporters in the Middle East. The subsequent hallmark New Zealand combat contributions of artillery in 1965, and of infantry in 1967, were decided after my tour of duty. Those commitments prompted establishment at last of a full-blown embassy in Saigon in 1967, with Paul Edmonds as the first resident New Zealand Ambassador. He had been deputy to Sir Stephen Weir in Bangkok. In my memory, he remains one of the most astute and discerning, if unorthodox, of New Zealand front-line diplomats.

Day-to-day preoccupations with the grindstone of the New Zealand aid programme in Vietnam conveyed little sense of involvement with a grand strategic plan to arrest the so-called domino theory, according to which the fall of Vietnam to iniquitous communist insurrection would inevitably condemn all Southeast Asia to the same fate. That big strategic concept was way beyond my pay grade. But it was not just hindsight that nourished a sense that deepening American intrusion was unwise in Vietnam, a country with severe post-colonial challenges to its unity and prosperity. I was occasionally involved in friendly discussion about this with American aid officials – some of whom concurred.

༄

Following the Bangkok assignment, my job pathway was redirected into different pastures. It was almost ten years before I returned to Asian preoccupations. The government of Norman Kirk had been elected in November 1972 with a slate of ambitious goals, including a more active foreign policy. Two aspects of that extended my personal Asian prelude: first, the establishment of resident diplomatic relations with China; second, the brave commitment to double New Zealand's foreign aid budget over just two years, with significant implications for aid policy, planning and management within what was now the Ministry of Foreign Affairs (the old title of Department of External Affairs had been dropped in 1968).

I was assigned as deputy to David McDowell (later to be head of the Prime Minister's Office), who was charged with implementing the new government's ambitious timetable for aid increases. The task involved much breaking of new ground and more extensive Ministry of Foreign Affairs (MFA) cooperation with other government departments, non-government agencies and individuals, as well as dedicated forward planning of commitments and disbursements to an extent not previously envisaged.

Beyond practical experience in Thailand and Vietnam as a lowly aid officer, I had minimal qualifications for overall aid policy planning. There was a very significant degree of learning on the job. I led different aid missions to Southeast Asia (Thailand, Philippines, Malaysia, Indonesia) and into the South Pacific.

But first, by way of an overture, was the opening of a New Zealand Embassy in Beijing, which the new Kirk Government had elevated into a priority. My responsibility here derived from an assignment to the MFA property section along with Michael Mansfield. The section was charged with acquiring and furnishing overseas properties. New Zealand ownership of the accommodation required for an expanding diplomatic network was also a declared objective of the Kirk administration. This was a high octane adventure entailing purchase by way of a fast-track authority of many new properties, most of which, although not all, proved sound enough acquisitions, but many of which were later sold off to balance MFA books at times of belt tightening, and as part of MFA compliance with cost accrual accounting driven out of the Treasury.

To establish an embassy physically in China we really were starting from ground zero, in a country about which New Zealand knew very little. As it was, I was only included at 72 hours' notice (following late withdrawal of a colleague) on the first New Zealand ministerial delegation to China, led by the Trade and Associate Foreign Minister Joe Walding in March 1973. My task was to liaise with Chinese authorities and arrange to secure premises for an embassy, for an ambassadorial residence and for staff accommodation. I also found myself designated as note-taker (by the senior Foreign Affairs official on the delegation, Bryce Harland, later to be New Zealand's first Ambassador to China) for the official discussions which Joe Walding held with various Chinese ministers. This was clearly a seminal moment for New Zealand external relations, although that sensation is obviously amplified by what has transpired in the New Zealand–China relationship over the nearly 50 years since. Hindsight cannot be denied.

The note-taking responsibility involved new experience. The participants at ministerial meetings were seated usually in a generous half circle of armchairs and sofas. It was difficult for a note-taker always to hear what was being said, although the requirement for English–Mandarin interpretation slowed proceedings appreciably, and note-taking was less fevered. It provided my first encounter with the presence of spittoons in international diplomacy. These unfamiliar receptacles were placed between each pair of armchairs, and the clearing of throats by our Chinese hosts throughout the exchanges soon explained their use. I waited with bated breath to witness a result – a distraction from note-taking.

The practical side of my task required visits with Chinese counterparts to the diplomatic enclave then under construction in Beijing, and to the apartment blocks where the Ambassador and staff would be housed until a residence was built. The Chinese informed me that New Zealand was on their 'A List' for an embassy building – along with Britain, Australia, Canada, etc. They showed me the actual site earmarked for New Zealand, where ground had already been turned and some preliminary construction begun.

I suggested to my Chinese counterparts that New Zealand's diplomatic service was considerably smaller than that of other designated A-Listers, and more modest premises would therefore suit our needs. This was politely but firmly resisted; the matter had been decided. At the time of writing, New Zealand has recently completed a rebuild of its Beijing Embassy. The size and appointments of the original, along with several modifications and additions over ensuing years, were plainly not sufficient for 21st-century New Zealand requirements; my original modesty proved to be misplaced.

Walding informed me, en route to Beijing, that he would be leading a large New Zealand trade mission to China four months hence, and it was essential that our embassy be functional by that time. This was a very big ask. I recall remarking to him that to set up a fully operational mission in just four months in Canberra would have been a real test, let alone Beijing.

On the eve of our final departure from China, and preparing for a farewell meeting with the Chinese Foreign Minister, Walding asked his delegation whether there were any points he should register with his host. I responded that if we were to meet a four-month deadline for an established embassy on the ground (even one functioning in temporary premises) then we would need to cut corners and seek permission from the Chinese to fly all basic furnishings and appointments into Beijing (I had been told that rail transport from Hong Kong to Beijing was notoriously unreliable). The only practical solution would be to enlist the help of the RNZAF to use their C-130 Hercules for transport.

I had been cautioned on all sides in Beijing that the Chinese simply did not allow foreign military aircraft to land at Beijing Airport. I suggested Walding might seek a special dispensation for New Zealand from the Chinese Foreign Minister. It was a pretty forlorn hope. Joe Walding produced a rabbit from the hat, however, when he informed me later that evening that the Foreign Minister had agreed to a New Zealand dispensation.

The task of establishing the Beijing mission completely monopolised my time once back in Wellington. The RNZAF were willing and able, but there was not time to put out to tender the supply of furnishings and labour, so the Wellington interior design firm Reesby Interiors was contracted. Furnishings for the office (desks, typewriters, paper, clips and binders) were secured through the department's own channels. Reesby supplied all domestic and other furnishings based upon floor plans (for an identified temporary office as well as private residences) supplied by the Chinese authorities. Reesby also assembled a team of tradespeople to paint, to lay the carpet, to hang wallpaper and curtaining, etc., all of them to be carried on the plane. This was in every sense a Herculean adventure. I do not know whether it was true but the RNZAF, who performed heroically, claimed later that they had in fact broken the world load record at that time for a C-130.

There were eleventh-hour alarms. I was in the garden of my Wellington home on a Saturday afternoon when I received word from the New Zealand office in Hong Kong that the Chinese authorities were now insisting that the C-130 – which was at that time in the air bound for Beijing – must land in Hong Kong and the cargo be discharged and forwarded by rail to Beijing. With dismay I contacted my senior in the department, Rod Miller, who with great calm instructed me to get our Hong Kong office to reassure the Chinese authorities that New Zealand was actively considering diplomatic visas for the advance party of Chinese diplomats (then waiting in Hong Kong) to travel to open China's embassy in Wellington, and it would be helpful if confirmation from the Chinese side was forthcoming that the C-130 now proceeding to Beijing would be allowed to land there, in accordance with earlier understandings. I admired this quiet bureaucratic brinkmanship but was personally very dubious. Later in the evening, to great relief on all sides, word came through from Hong Kong that the C-130 was now en route direct to Beijing. Its landing at the airport was a first in New Zealand–China relations.

My memory of the Walding expedition is dominated by impressions of thousands upon thousands of cyclists everywhere on the main city thoroughfares, all dressed alike in Mao style, with an occasional truck or bus but hardly a car. There was no colour amongst the drab crowds. The New Zealand delegation was housed in the former US legation in Beijing, a handsome collection of buildings with a pleasant garden, which the Chinese used as a government guest house. The delegation became the object of curiosity, particularly from children, when out walking the streets, especially beyond Beijing. One port of call was an overnight in Wuhan where an enormous throng of Chinese school children lined the streets waving miniature New Zealand flags as the Walding cavalcade drove past. In those times Wuhan was famous as the place where Mao swam the Yangtze River.

Joe Walding proved a good choice for the pathbreaking role. He was a reputed gastronome (his physique confirmed it) and the combination of his shrewd mind, indefatigable enthusiasms and trencherman capacities proved just what was needed. He conspicuously and consistently outperformed the New Zealand delegation and its accompanying media group at the copious dinners, lunches, receptions and breakfasts generously offered by Chinese hosts everywhere. One particular highlight was an official dinner attended by Chinese Premier Zhou Enlai, to whom we were all introduced. The NZPA journalist Derek Round, a member of the accompanying New Zealand media party, 'rescued' the chopsticks used by Zhou at the meal, and presented them as a momento to Walding.

The return included travel by scheduled overnight train from Wuhan to Canton (now Guangzhou). The delegation travelled in a specially attached last carriage with a VIP compartment containing a small four-poster bed and a striking antique copper hip bath. Walding revelled in these surroundings, insisting upon a photo of himself in the bath. The carriage also contained a dining room, armchairs, a copiously stocked drinks cabinet, and an open verandah with elegant wickerwork chairs, where we sat and gazed as the vastness of China slid by. The New Zealand Minister was in his element.

He had one last trick. Upon return to Hong Kong he suggested the delegation, plus members of the New Zealand office there, join him in his suite at the Mandarin Hotel to wind down after the expedition. It was a convivial occasion with plenty of refreshment. At one point the telephone rang. The call was taken by the Minister's Private Secretary Brian Bremner, who announced to Mr Walding that there was a *New York Times* journalist in the lobby asking for an interview. The Minister responded he was not in the mood for such a thing.

Bryce Harland, who remained perhaps the most composed of the assembled New Zealand team, remonstrated that this seemed too good an opportunity to pass up. The *New York Times* was, after all, an authoritative journal and its coverage would be valuable. Walding retorted by suggesting Harland himself talk with the journalist, but the latter asserted the contact had really to come from the Minister. With a twinkle in his eye, Walding responded to Harland, 'You pretend to be me, and I will pretend to be you.' There were murmurs of bibulous assent from the attendant revellers.

So it was. Walding wove his way to the door when the journalist arrived and intoned that he was 'Mr Harland, the Minister's principal adviser', and ushered her to an alcove in the suite, where he introduced her to the seated New Zealand 'Minister'. The ensuing interview was fairly brief but serious. At the other end of the room the assembled celebrants suppressed their hilarity, with difficulty, until the journalist's departure. It was never clear whether the *New York Times* actually carried a piece on the interview, but as it is America's respected journal of record there may be something hidden somewhere in a distant archive.

CR

Property Section involved work on the home front too. In 1973 the component parts of External Affairs were spread through three or four different buildings across central Wellington – this included the top floor of Parliament Buildings, where the Secretary and Deputy Secretaries remained. As the new broom of the Kirk Government swept clean, responsibilities were thrust upon the Property Section to find new premises where the entire Ministry of Foreign Affairs could be housed. After much searching and planning space allocation, the Ministry was moved lock, stock and barrel into Dalmuir House on The Terrace in Wellington. The senior executives, however, stuck hard, insisting they remain at Parliament with ready access to the Prime Minister. This infuriated the State Services Commission, and their disfavour bedevilled the lowly Property Section, the meat in the sandwich, as it strove to effect the move to new premises.

My second responsibility was to prepare an architect's brief for a new stand-alone Ministry building to be constructed behind Parliament on Hill Street, near to where the British High Commission now stands and adjacent to the motorway flyover. I had no qualifications at all for this responsibility but soon learnt that an architect's brief required extended consultation with architects, public service planners and ministerial colleagues about requirements to support and manage New Zealand's overseas representation and interests – looking out over a 50-year period ahead. Inflated dreams and flights of fancy interspersed with practical judgement informed the process. Eventually architectural plans for a low-rise three-storied building, with emphasis on horizontal not vertical coordination, were produced. As I readied to move to overseas aid work the plans all looked good on paper, and the drawings formed a wall display for departmental staff to admire.

The plans presumably still lie somewhere collecting dust in the archives. Nearly 50 years later it is instructive to reflect that MFAT remains a Wellington orphan with no permanent home. Rhetorical claims by successive New Zealand governments about commitment to an independent New Zealand foreign policy have never translated into support for independent Wellington accommodation. In contrast, New Zealand's security, intelligence and defence agencies have all acquired stand-alone accommodations. That reflects perhaps the priority now extended to security and intelligence factors in international relations, promoted especially by New Zealand's large and powerful partners and friends since the profound shock of the spectacular 9/11 terrorist attacks upon the American homeland, just as the present century began. The realities of New Zealand's situation, in particular the complete absence of real 'hard' power, require that diplomacy remains New Zealand's first specification in international relations. Intelligence does not make foreign policy; it supplements it. The furnishing of custom-built facilities for administration of New Zealand's modern international relations and foreign policy are a logical and valid premise.

CR

The Kirk Government's reinvigorated and expanded New Zealand aid effort, beginning in 1973, added dimensions to New Zealand's international relations, especially in Asia but also in the South Pacific, where New Zealand associations and commitments were of longer standing. It involved New Zealand as well in greater collective effort by donors to improve principles governing aid and its administration inside institutions like the World Bank or the Paris-based Organisation for Economic Co-operation and Development (OECD). The practice of peer group assessment of individual donors' performance by such bodies was a particular new departure.

New Zealand did not, like most donors at that time, formally tie its aid to the use of New Zealand goods or services, and its decisions on operational implementation were, on the whole, less protracted than those of many other donor countries. This was appreciated by recipient governments, who were often frustrated (as they remain today) at aid donor 'red tape'. At the Wellington end, inside the External Aid Division, effective delivery of New Zealand's assistance relied very much upon the competence and enthusiasms of individual desk officers, who were recruited in increasing numbers. Some projects, like imaginative support for Sir Edmund Hillary's Nepal schools programme, were products of that energy and industry.

Foundations were also laid at this time for New Zealand projects that successfully engaged the New Zealand private sector, like geothermal development in Indonesia and the Philippines, and construction of the Papua New Guinea parliament buildings. Some ventures were less noteworthy, like a beef development project for Thai tribespeople, which collapsed after the recipients consumed the stud animals gifted to start the programme, and construction of an abattoir in Laos that did not actually succeed in slaughtering a single animal.

The practice of aid conditionality, whereby aid recipients had to agree to the donor's specified conditions (e.g. the embrace of democracy) as the price for the aid, came under greater scrutiny. Hesitations grew over time, within reputable circles, about the actual viability of such conditionality. The emergence of successful new fast-growth economies, especially in Asia and most especially in China, moreover cast different light upon traditional conditionality. The lessons from their own manifestly successful economic progress pointed away from some accepted aid orthodoxy.

Expansion of the New Zealand aid effort widened the exposure of ministry officials to New Zealand special interest groups. They often espoused values, like human rights or sound environmental stewardship, that were directly relevant to the business of aid giving. Indeed such groups often possessed deeper understanding than government officials of issues and needs in individual recipient countries. This is of course conventional wisdom in today's world. But in those early years of New Zealand ODA expansion such lessons had to be learnt.

The broader question of how or whether New Zealand external aid should be uncoupled from New Zealand foreign policy, and conducted separately as a stand-alone professional activity, was not at that time quite such an issue as it subsequently became. Different donor countries have chosen different pathways. Given the primary focus of New Zealand's aid upon the South Pacific, and given the intrinsic political complexion of many New Zealand relationships with Pacific Island countries, there remains an undeniable political element to New Zealand aid policy in that region. At the time of writing, the professionalism of the contemporary New Zealand aid effort exceeds by a considerable margin the policies and the performance of those adolescent years, but whether aid should be an extension of New Zealand foreign policy or a stand-alone enterprise grounded in developmental priorities and social principles remains, nonetheless, a perennial topic.

When leading the first New Zealand aid mission to the soon-to-be fully independent Papua New Guinea (PNG) in 1975, politics were immediately front and centre. We were welcomed amicably by the PNGers, principally because we were not Australians. On the other hand, we were cautioned by high-ranking Australians on the ground to be careful about which aid projects New Zealand should undertake: Australia had its own priorities, and duplication of effort was to be absolutely avoided. That was fair enough. Australia's interests and extensive reach throughout meant PNG was by far the largest recipient of Australian largesse. The reality of politics in the business of aid could not be denied.

I was included too in an aid delegation to the Cook Islands, led by Bernie Galvin of Treasury. This was the first aid mission to the Cooks following dissolution by the Kirk Government of the old Department of Island Territories (yet another of its radical changes) and bestowal of responsibility for conduct of New Zealand's Cook Islands relationship upon External Affairs. It was a move intended to reflect a new maturity in dealings between the Cook Islands and New Zealand. Politics and aid were by design inevitably connected. Although I was not aware of it at the time, that particular relationship was to become a personal preoccupation before long.

3. EUROPEAN PREOCCUPATIONS

The yo-yo nature of involvement with New Zealand's external interests was amply confirmed over the first ten years of my apprenticeship. My original Bangkok experience had marked the beginning of an Asian episode, but it was followed immediately by a zig-zag into European and trade policy work. My return to Wellington from Asia in February 1965 proved short-lived; after barely 18 months I was posted, at six weeks' notice, to London. This was a complete surprise, occasioned by the late withdrawal of a colleague who was due to take up the post of Second Secretary at the London High Commission in the economic branch under the Economic Counsellor, the aforementioned Bernie Galvin – later to become Secretary to the Treasury and Head of the Prime Minister's Department.

Elizabeth's and my number one priority in Wellington had been to find a home. With financial assistance from the old State Advances Corporation, and after patient searching, we found and purchased in the suburb of Kelburn, a fairly typical house at the bottom of 45 steps. It required restoration but we believed we would have the time to complete that, when suddenly word came down from on high to move off shore once again.

Before the move I had spent a period in in the Economic Division of External Affairs involving work with the Cabinet Secretary (Ray Perry) as note-taker for the Cabinet Economic Committee. This modest role provided my first exposure to senior ministers who were to cross the path of my subsequent career, notably Deputy Prime Minister John Marshall and Finance Minister Robert Muldoon. Marshall's quiet, firm but almost courtly manner contrasted distinctly with Muldoon's bare-knuckle deportment, particularly whenever he became critical, as he often did, of senior economic officials in attendance. I was impressed by the way the Cabinet Secretary was able to deftly modulate my own inadequate draft record of Committee discussions and decisions so as to better reflect the intentions ministers really had (or ought to have had) in mind.

CR

The London apprenticeship proved stimulating. Bernie Galvin was a refreshing boss, less concerned with the etiquette or niceties of diplomacy than with practical hard-nosed economic interests. His main British counterpart in the Foreign and Commonwealth Office (FCO), Ken Gallagher, was a smooth, suave, fine-spoken official in black jacket and pinstripe trousers. The contrast between the two in action could not have been greater – but they shared a mutual respect. Gallagher inhabited a small venerable room in Whitehall from another age, with an open fireplace replenished during wintertime meetings by a minion shuffling in and out bearing a coal bucket to stoke the fire.

The Economic Branch at the High Commission had two closely connected objectives. First, sustaining levels of permitted exports (dairy, meat, fruit, etc.) to the British market under a 1958 duty-free access agreement: a legacy of World War II arrangements and times of desperate British need for New Zealand food supplies. Secondly, shadowing progress of the British Government's professed intention to join the European Economic Community (EEC), as it was then known. As suggested earlier, looking backwards from the present time at this all-consuming New Zealand obsession of 50 years ago, it seems to belong to another world entirely.

A formal British application to join Europe had first been lodged in 1961, but it was rejected by a French veto two years later. It was clear when I arrived at the High Commission in 1966 that a second British bid was imminent, under a different British government (led by Harold Wilson) and it was duly lodged in May 1967. It was once again vetoed by the French after barely six months. But it was crystal clear that Whitehall was not about to give up, and the New Zealand High Commission disposed its efforts accordingly. The third and ultimately successful application was lodged in June 1970. By that time I had been moved (once more at very short notice) to a different foxhole on the battlefield, and was totally immersed in Brussels with the prospects and complexities for New Zealand of the British application.

In several ways the London High Commission was a microcosm of Wellington bureaucracy itself. In 1966 there were some 35–40 New Zealand-seconded staff: representatives of the railways, the public trust, science, tourism, public relations, migration and agriculture, as well as military attachés and trade and political staff, all under the High Commissioner Tom Macdonald – a somewhat remote figure from my everyday existence. Some of the public relations staff had been fixtures at the High Commission for many years. They were timeworn, comfortably settled in their own ways, and they seemed to regard foreign and trade officers as transient birds of passage, whilst they provided the indispensable ballast and a network of (traditional) contacts for the High Commission. It was all a bit old fashioned.

On the other hand, New Zealand House itself was only seven years old and, with its shine and gloss, still an architectural landmark for London. Like the city itself, much has changed since. The staff has been slimmed, quite rightly, while the building looks its age, given economies in maintenance over the years, and as London has adorned itself with much attractive modern architecture. With penthouse views over Horse Guards Parade, Whitehall and St James' Park, New Zealand House was popular with visitors, and seconded staff, even junior ones, could avail themselves of the penthouse to offer hospitality to Whitehall contacts. Because of its central location and the scenic rooftop, a good turnout of targeted guests was a reasonable bet.

The compensations of a London posting at the time included an accommodation allowance for High Commission staff that was sufficient to enable Elizabeth and I to rent a small terrace up/down house just off the King's Road in Chelsea, with its reputation as one of London's nifty spaces. We were very lucky. It took 40–45 minutes to walk to New Zealand House, which provided daily exercise past some London landmarks – Sloane Square, Eaton Square, Buckingham Palace, St James' Park, the Mall, the Duke of York Steps, Pall Mall and the Haymarket. All very evocative. In the evening, the number 19 bus from Haymarket to Chelsea provided the return journey.

My apprenticeship in London provided exposure for the first time to Whitehall and the style of negotiation at the FCO, the Board of Trade and the Ministry of Agriculture. At the FCO there was frequently an air of slight condescension, evasion and sense of superior accomplishment. Both there and at the Board of Trade there was a propensity amongst senior officials to spell out for the High Commission just where New Zealand best interests might lie when it came to the hard bargaining of the terms of British EEC entry. As a junior spear carrier and note-taker, I cheered silently at the quiet, composed, non-deferential approach of our Secretary of Trade and Industry Jim Moriarty during his forays to London, as he clearly but politely reassured British mandarins across the table that, when push came to shove, New Zealand could be counted on to define its national interest.

The business of keeping track of British preparations for a possible negotiation with the EEC was painstaking. These were the days before 24-hour television news, Google, Wikipedia, emails, Twitter and the like. Each morning careful inspection of numerous daily newspapers, and each week of the relevant magazines, was obligatory. Editorials were collected about the EEC and the issues Britain would have to contend with in negotiation. One could not even confidently rely upon receipt of press releases from British Cabinet ministers' offices. As a result the texts of ministerial or senior official statements, as well as the views of captains of industry and, most important, leaders of the UK farming community, had to be hunted down, particularly when statements were delivered outside London.

Frequently one only learnt about such material at second or third hand, before setting off on a goose chase. All or most of the information was conveyed by cable to Wellington, with an interpretation from the High Commission's standpoint where appropriate. Reports of major British political statements were of course often carried by the wire services like Reuters or the NZPA, who had a correspondent in London, but rarely the complete texts; and for New Zealand the devil lay, as it always has, in the detail.

The line preached to Wellington out of the High Commission on Britain's EEC ambition was that despite French obstructionism the wisest course for New Zealand throughout was to presume that ultimately the British would succeed. This judicial fatalism was a conclusion which Wellington itself had also made, so they hardly needed a reminder. Back in 1963 when President Charles de Gaulle of France had flatly rejected

Britain's first bid there had, however, been a palpable New Zealand sense of reprieve.

Once new British Prime Minister Harold Wilson commenced, in January 1967, scoping the issues for resolution by Britain and Europe in an eventual second negotiation, he began with progressive tours of EEC capitals. The need for prior understanding between the British and ourselves about the actual dimensions of New Zealand's problem, and the form of necessary solutions, became vital. Visits to London by New Zealand ministers, officials and producer board chairmen intensified. My role – as note-taker at a copious number of such exchanges with British officials and ministers, and as preparer of first drafts of reporting cables to Wellington for perusal and finalisation by Bernie Galvin – was the start of a total immersion in the complexities of key New Zealand external economic interests which lasted about 20 years. At the bottom line, New Zealand faced a situation where crucial aspects of the country's future and wellbeing were to be determined by a British–European negotiation from which New Zealand itself would be physically excluded.

There were, nonetheless, welcome diversions from British–EEC matters, such as observing and reporting on the annual Conservative Party conference in Blackpool, attending the Farnborough Airshow in company with the High Commission's military attachés, and representing New Zealand at the International Whaling Commission (IWC) in London. That last provided a cautionary lesson.

New Zealand had ceased whaling in 1964 and the issue had not yet become quite the controversial matter internationally that it became in subsequent years. At the time IWC membership consisted, from memory, of some 28 member governments. A laconic two-line cable in 1967 from Wellington informed the High Commission that there would be no representative sent from New Zealand for the upcoming annual meeting, at which whale catch quotas were to be decided; it suggested that the High Commission step into the breach and that New Zealand representation should be a two-person delegation consisting of Paul Cotton, who was a First Secretary, and myself. The instruction added in the same breath that there had been no opportunity to prepare a detailed briefing, but the New Zealand delegation should vote in favour of the lowest catch quota proposed at the meeting.

The absence of background guidance limited the contribution which the tenderfoot New Zealand team could actually offer when horse trading about alternative quota packages began, as it did straight away behind the scenes. The assembled delegations comprised a cast of battle-hardened whaling practitioners and policy makers. Our delegation of amateurs was, to put it baldly, disregarded.

The political backdrop to the meeting, of course, was the Cold War between the Soviet-led Communist bloc and the US-led Western nations. On the final morning of the meeting several quota proposals lay on the table, including one from the Soviet Union which was for the lowest permissible catch of all the proposals. Our instructions were crystal clear, so when the vote was called as the very first item on the agenda, we placed the New Zealand ballot accordingly in support of Moscow, only to discover we had tiptoed behind the Soviet Union onto thin ice.

The Chair announced there were just two in favour of the Russian proposal (the Soviet Union and New Zealand) and 26 against (the rest of the membership). The Soviets had calculated privately, we then learnt, that their national share of the overall catch quota would not be diminished, even were that overall quota figure itself to be reduced. Other delegations were fully seized of the devious Soviet grandstanding behind its proposal; the New Zealand delegation was not. An alternative proposal supported by the US and the rest of the membership finally carried the day.

By chance, that evening the Soviet Embassy in London hosted a large reception for the IWC. As Paul Cotton and I entered, the Ambassador and Soviet delegation leader plus supporting staff advanced noisily to embrace us at the entrance, summoning a waiter with a tray of vodka and caviar while severally and ostentatiously we toasted mutual friendship. A stonefaced assembly of IWC delegates looked disapprovingly on. Reprimand was in the air. Paul and I swiftly repaired to the High Commission to prepare a cabled report for Wellington in an attempt to whitewash our dereliction of Cold War duty.

ભ

Given the EEC preoccupations at the High Commission there was logic, I supposed, behind Wellington's decision, at very short notice, to cross-post me in 1968 to Brussels. It was, yet again, a surprise. The prescribed tour of duty for my position at the High Commission had been three to four years, but I had by then barely served two years in the Haymarket.

The Brussels office was small by London standards. It had the dual function of Embassy to Belgium (and to Luxembourg) as well as New Zealand Mission to the EEC. The latter responsibility monopolised attention, although trade with Belgium, especially in wool for its carpet industry, was important and a trade commissioner, Fergus McLean, was among the six seconded staff, three of whom covered EEC matters. That included the Ambassador, Merv Norrish, later to become Ambassador to Washington and then Permanent Head of the Ministry of Foreign Affairs.

Plucked from a modest rank at the London High Commission, I was lucky now to be Merv Norrish's deputy, with rank of First Secretary. The third officer with EEC responsibility was Roger Kerr, who subsequently cut a figure as Executive Director of the New Zealand Business Roundtable in the 1980s and 1990s, an arch apostle of neo-liberal free-market thinking; he became a convinced participant in the international neo-liberal conclave the Mont Pelerin Society. The philosophy behind key European policies was hardly from the free-market playbook, particularly when it came to farm trade, and during his tenure Roger struggled sometimes in interactions with EEC Commission officials.

The Embassy was situated on one floor of an office block in the Rue de la Loi, a gloomy, noisy, one-way thoroughfare that linked the large European Commission headquarters at Berlaymont (which were at that stage still under construction) to the inner ring-road around the Brussels city centre. The din of traffic was constant. Belgians at the time, while requiring a licence to drive, had no requirement to pass any test. Many had never had a formal driving lesson in their lives. Noisy Belgian road behaviour (the horn was as important as the accelerator) penetrated our office, and compounded the difficulties of newcomers adjusting to the left-hand rule of the road. We also had to adjust to Belgium's division into a Flemish (Dutch-speaking) north and a Walloon (French-speaking) south. Brussels itself sits at the dividing line between the two communities. The suburb where Elizabeth and I rented our first home, Rhode-Saint-Genèse (near the Waterloo battlefield), was right at the front line, with Flemish spoken at the shops but French on the buses and trams.

Our arrival in Brussels in May 1968 coincided with a massive general strike south of the border in France, an hour by road from Brussels, whose impact convulsed the whole of Europe. Widespread student and worker protest over social and economic conditions dominated TV screens. French President Charles de Gaulle survived the upheaval, but only just – and he resigned the following year. The relevance of all this to New Zealand's interests lay of course in the indisputable influence that France wielded inside the EEC. De Gaulle had, after all, twice vetoed British entry.

Were British prospects for a successful third bid improved or not by the French turmoil and de Gaulle's disappearance? The new President, Georges Pompidou, was rumoured to be more amenable. A third British application was duly lodged in June 1970 by a new, staunchly pro-EEC Conservative British government in Whitehall, led by Edward Heath. After 12 months of complex negotiation that utterly consumed the life of the New Zealand Brussels Mission, this bid eventually succeeded in June 1971.

In 1968 the most pressing preoccupation for the Europeans (and by extension for New Zealand) was the roll out of the key components of the EEC Common Agricultural Policy (CAP), involving a cascade of intricate, definitive regulations covering the sectors of dairy, meat, fruit, cereals, etc., all of which Britain would be obliged to accept as the price of EEC membership. These had been negotiated long and hard between the six member states and the EEC Commission, under the energetic leadership of the Commissioner for Agriculture, Sicco Mansholt. Myth had it that Mansholt first sketched the basic provisions one lunchtime on a Brussels restaurant tablecloth, which now occupied an honoured place within EEC headquarters.

Hard and quick learning by New Zealand was obviously required. The first challenge was language. All documents were in French, the lingua franca of the European Community (although the languages of the other five member states were also official). On top of this the provisions were couched in the entirely new intrusive vocabulary of European agriculture; they spoke of intervention prices, threshold prices, sluice gate prices, variable levies, export restitutions, and much more. To comprehend this forbidding vocabulary of regulation and centralised management in English, let alone French, presented a challenge. There were no websites, no Google, no technological gizmos to explain, simplify or interpret.

There had been no language training offered to brush up or improve my limited French language ability, given the quick transfer to Brussels. Listening assiduously to the radio, reading French-language newspapers with a dictionary in one hand, and a process of rote learning quickly became standard necessity. I could, after a while, conduct and argue by heart the case for fair treatment for New Zealand well enough in French, but everyday social conversation was more of a stretch. My English translations of copious EEC regulations, duly forwarded to Wellington, always bore, as a precaution, in heavy print 'This Is An Unofficial Translation'.

Precise and swift instructions from Wellington to the Mission frequently ensued, seeking clarification or registering robust New Zealand misgivings about sundry technical provisions. This deepened my unease about the accuracy of amateur translation. The Ministry in Wellington now provides more comprehensive language training to its officers posted to Francophone countries, entailing study in congenial surroundings in the sunny south of France – a marked and enviable improvement.

The European Commission had, by 1968, been in existence just ten years. My impressions of the first generation of officials and advisers were of competence and visible sense of purpose. Many plainly believed they were engaged in serious transformation of Europe – putting behind rivalries, disagreements and conflicts of the past. Some of the policies (like agriculture) were distinctly unpalatable to New Zealand and other outsiders, but there could be no doubt about the convictions, skills and abilities amongst the proponents.

When I went back to Brussels 12 years later as Ambassador, English was an official language, which greatly eased problems of comprehension. Inside the European Commission, however, some of the original vitality had ebbed. Many of the officials (which now of course included British, Irish and Danish in their ranks) seemed somewhat prosaic, even defensive, about the European Community's existence and its prospects.

Whether this was true or not, it was essential that New Zealand cultivated Commission contacts, before and after the British entry negotiations, across a broad front – involving both those officials in the engine room, charged with actually writing first drafts of new or changed rules for European agriculture, and those at more elevated levels, concerned with grander issues of trade and external relations policy. Those last included the European Commissioners themselves, who formed a sort of cabinet at the top of the tree. The latter remained targets principally for the Ambassador, but wining and dining at all levels was a dedicated task. Some of the more technical Commission staff, so it was claimed, discreetly checked bottle labels for the quality of wine being offered before deciding how much they might divulge to the host.

Journalists were also a particular target. The quality and skill of the large Brussels press corps was exceptional. That was not a surprise given the stakes involved with negotiations for the entry and subsequent membership of Britain (in tandem with those of Ireland and Denmark). Once the negotiations finally got going in earnest in 1970, the role of the media became paramount as they reported each twist and turn. Spin doctors from the participating European delegations came into their element, feeding the journalists with their dogma.

There was advantage for the New Zealand Mission to join the journalist throng in the corridors during the long hours of negotiation, even when issues on the table might not specifically concern New Zealand. Such practice helped absorb the chemistry of the process, and helped judge progress being made by the British entry negotiators across the board. That was important because the issue of when to press hard and when to pedal softly on New Zealand's vital concerns was a judgement call which preoccupied New Zealand policy makers throughout in their contacts with the British negotiators.

Formally speaking, British debriefing about progress with the negotiations occurred in London with embassy and high commission staff of the concerned countries there. It proved important, however, that New Zealand double-check through its network of European embassies, and at EEC headquarters, to seek assessments from the European side about progress and tactics. Not surprisingly, these shades of opinion and interpretation contrasted at times with those volunteered in London. It was quite understandable that in London, British debriefers would alway be concerned to put a constructive gloss on proceedings and conclusions.

The 12 months of the entry negotiations proper (1970–1971) were characterised throughout by conspicuous leaking in Brussels of documents and position papers. The European Commission retained first responsibility for preparing policy position papers for the European governments. The chief Commission negotiator supervising British entry was a skilled Frenchman, Jean-François Deniau (just as another such Frenchman, Michel Barnier, negotiated Britain's exit 45 years later). His statements, his asides and his body language were keenly scrutinised by all inside the Brussels bubble.

Friendly Commission contacts, after accepting hospitality, would slip internal documents directly or indirectly to the New Zealand Mission. These could be traded with other missions and with journalists in return for yet more information obtained by others from their respective contacts. This flourishing black market meant that on occasion the New Zealand Mission was able to secure important position papers, directly relevant to solutions for New Zealand, in advance of their circulation to the European negotiators themselves. British documents fell into New Zealand hands in the same way. The cultivation of the admirable and influential Brussels press corps paid off. This cultivation involved the offer of fully funded visits to New Zealand for individual French, German and British journalists as part of Wellington's dedicated programme, aimed at winning understanding and support for the New Zealand cause.

In June 1970 the prospects for British success were improved by the election of Georges Pompidou as French President. The negotiating pace in Brussels immediately quickened. This certainly did not mean that France would not continue to drive a hard bargain; indeed Paris declined formally to recognise that New Zealand's vital interests required any special arrangement. For the French, the New Zealand problem was one for Britain alone to resolve, and London would be required to accept, in full and from the outset, European rules on agriculture and everything else – even if a transitional period for actual adjustment were granted.

The considerable New Zealand energy and effort expended to gain political recognition at the highest levels in European capitals and in London, and the dimensions and solutions of the New Zealand problems, are captured in Volume 2 of Sir John Marshall's *Memoirs*, covering the years 1960–1988. He recounts there in detail intensive exchanges with leaders in Europe and also in the US. His perseverance and steady demeanour, together with an ability to invest the presentation of the New Zealand case to European capitals and to the British (where he acquired a media profile) with fresh immediacy during a campaign that lasted in effect over a whole decade, was prodigious.

It is a pity that there remains, after all these years, no well researched authoritative public study of the New Zealand experience with British EEC entry, although one or two doctoral theses and some academic writing have been devoted to the New Zealand campaign. One readable journalistic account is NZPA correspondent Mike Robson's *Decision at Dawn: New Zealand and the EEC*, published in paperback in 1972 by Bayard-Hillier. The 2008 autobiography *Against the Odds* (Dunmore Press) by Ted Woodfield, New Zealand's leading trade policy official for at least part of the British entry saga, provides a chronicle of events. It pays less regard, however, to the role of New Zealand's European embassies in actually keeping doors open and consistently disseminating New Zealand's message to ministers, commissioners, senior officials and media throughout the EEC capitals.

It is important to recall that over those same years there were serious competing issues that consumed policy makers and advisers in Wellington – in particular New Zealand's involvement in the Vietnam War. That subject has rightly attracted New Zealand historians and others, in contrast to the largely unrecorded EEC enlargement experience. Yet it was the latter that energised shifts not just in New Zealand trade patterns, but also in foreign relations, as successive New Zealand governments sought new political ties over the generation ahead that were indispensable to diversification of New Zealand's export economy.

It was felicitous that when the final curtain fell in Luxembourg in June 1971, and the New Zealand solution was agreed in the form of the so-called Luxembourg Protocol 18 to the British entry treaty, John Marshall was one of only three ministers present amongst the mighty throng who had been involved right from the outset in the decade-long British entry saga. That durability surely counted in New Zealand's favour.

As the final UK–EEC ministerial negotiations came down to the wire in June 1971, we had taken practical precautions to book Luxembourg hotel space, which was under great pressure – so much so that John Marshall and his accompanying officials were installed nearly 20 kilometres outside the city in a hotel at Mondorf-les-Bains (this was the hotel where bigwig Nazi war criminals Hermann Göring and company had been lodged before the post–World War II Nuremberg trials). I was fortunate to have access to accommodation in a central Luxembourg apartment belonging to a French friend working at the European Parliament. We also acquired an office at the Grand Cravat Hotel in central Luxembourg as a base. British negotiators, who called variously (and sometimes furtively) to liaise throughout proceedings, proved leery lest the New Zealand base was bugged. As it was, a cloak-and-dagger quality prevailed, involving discreet shuttling of John Marshall to and from the site of the actual negotiation at the Kirchberg building on the outskirts of Luxembourg city. Switching cars and side-door entry was the order of the day (and night) in order to avoid the exuberant rolling maul of journalists.

Marshall emphasised in contacts with Geoffrey Rippon, the British Minister for EEC negotiations, that he stood in the wings to help the British secure the best entry terms possible, not as a sideline critic. But in an eleventh-hour BBC interview to the British equivalent of Radio New Zealand's *Morning Report*, given just before leaving London for the Luxembourg showdown, Marshall had described proposals to safeguard New Zealand's position, as they then lay on the table, as insufficient. This produced caustic reaction amongst Rippon's senior Foreign Office advisers in Luxembourg, headed by the redoubtable mandarin Sir Con O'Neill, who paid a terse early call on Marshall at the Cravat Hotel. But Rippon himself, a fellow lawyer, acknowledged Marshall's own description of the role as 'helper' and went back into the negotiation chamber to try to secure improvement.

Around 4.00 am on 21 June 1971, Rippon arrived unbidden at the Cravat to inform Marshall about what lay finally on the negotiating table back at the Kirchberg. He professed fatigue and announced he had not eaten for many hours. The Cravat restaurant and room service were long since closed, and all Luxembourg eateries were shut down tight. The New Zealand delegation was able only to rustle up some elderly sandwiches belonging to one of the New Zealand Mission drivers, M. Julin, prepared by his wife the day before. He willingly parted with them. Marshall and Rippon chomped away, and 'M. Julin's sandwiches' became thus a small footnote to New Zealand–EEC folklore.

I passed a large part of the night in the Kirchberg corridors amongst the journalists and the spin doctors who consistently fed the media pack, as news trickled out from the negotiating chamber. I kept the New Zealand delegation at the Cravat informed by telephone and fielded journalists' questions about New Zealand's interests and expectations. On at least one occasion the British Foreign Office spin doctor exhorted me to quit the pack assembled around him at a British press briefing. As dawn broke, with finality reached, champagne was broken out amongst the large scrum of exhausted journalists and negotiators. In the morning Rippon flew back to London on a special plane, carrying Marshall on board. Photos of their arrival at London in the British press were intended to signify an outcome agreeable to both parties.

In straight-out figures the New Zealand solution formula permitted continued access for New Zealand butter to the United Kingdom at 165,000 tonnes in 1973, declining to 138,000 tonnes by 1977; and for cheese at 68,000 tonnes in 1973, decreasing to 15,000 tonnes by 1977. What would happen at the end of these five years was an issue left for another day. It would clearly require yet more inexorable petitioning. The outcome amounted to a stay of execution, not a final reprieve. But it was nonetheless significant. I never imagined for a moment that I would be back for a repeat performance.

Among the lessons from the decade-long slog of British EEC entry was that megaphone diplomacy did not cut the mustard for New Zealand, given its limited leverage. Australia had opted publicly for strident combativeness throughout the British negotiations, but in the end Canberra secured virtually nothing. That led to a rather typical piece of official trans-Tasman embroidery to the effect that Australia had, in the end, magnanimously stood aside to permit a solution for New Zealand.

Throughout the British negotiations with Europe, New Zealand ministers and officials had conjured 'soft power' arguments to support the New Zealand cause – well before the notion gained currency in the language of international relations. For those American realists who coined the term, 'soft power' was the twin side of a coin with 'hard power'. America has possessed both, of course, in spades. The idea, however, that smaller countries might, in the total absence of hard power, also dispose of soft power and employ it in an essentially protective sense, never registered with American realists.

The New Zealand 'soft power' refrain intoned to Europeans was that of a small unthreatening Western democracy with shared culture, values, ties of kith and kin, and a record of battlefield sacrifice on European soil. It propounded too that, as an efficient food producer in a hungry world, it made no sense to damage such New Zealand potential as the price of European unity. Calculated appeals to European self esteem posed the question of how an enlarged Europe could ever hope to deal successfully with major economic powers like the United States or Japan if it could not accommodate the vital interests of a responsible friendly democracy like New Zealand.

Language played a key part in arriving at the accommodation for New Zealand interests. Wordsmiths occupied the driver's seat throughout. At the outset New Zealand had championed (with tongue in cheek) a formula of continued 'free and unrestricted access' to the UK market inside the EEC. The British resisted that language as wholly unrealistic. New Zealand then advocated 'comparable outlets' in an enlarged EEC, equivalent to those it enjoyed in the UK. The Europeans resisted that. The EEC made it clear (at French prompting, very early in the negotiations proper) that degressive transitional arrangements were the only option on offer to New Zealand and that these would terminate at the end of a British entry transition period (1973–1977). New Zealand wordsmiths countered with language to make the case for 'permanent' arrangements. The EEC flatly repudiated that notion. New Zealand then tried a formulation providing for an 'enduring arrangement'. This was also rebuffed, as was the formula of 'a continuing arrangement subject to review'. Finally a 'transitional arrangement subject to review' supplied the words acceptable to all sides. This struggle over 'studied ambiguity' extended throughout the 12 months of the negotiations.

There were amusing sidelights to the all-intrusive New Zealand trade access issues in Brussels life. One involved a painting by New Zealand's notable artist Frances Hodgkins, which hung on the wall at the British Ambassador's residence in Brussels. At a dinner attended by our Ambassador, Merv Norrish, the conversation turned to the fine paintings displayed on the walls, lent to the Foreign Office by art galleries such as the Tate and the National Gallery in London for display in British embassies overseas. The British Ambassador admitted how fortunate he was to live surrounded by such admirable art. He added that indeed amongst the selection there was only one that his wife and he disliked, by someone called Hodgkins. Norrish observed that Frances Hodgkins was indeed an esteemed New Zealand painter, and if ever the British wished to dispose of that painting, he was reasonably sure the New Zealand authorities would be interested to acquire it.

It subsequently transpired the British Ambassador had then actually written to the Foreign Office in London in these terms and received a stern reply to the effect it was not accepted practice to dispose of artwork in the way the Ambassador seemed to suggest. Nothing daunted, he had then responded to the effect that since the UK was on the verge of a major negotiation to join Europe, and the problems of New Zealand presented a particular difficulty, a gesture in respect to the Kiwis in the form of Hodgkins' painting might be regarded as a sweetener. It was in that spirit he had made his original suggestion. The Foreign Office thanked the Ambassador for his cogent explanation, and agreed New Zealand could purchase the painting for the price originally paid for it some 20 years previously, which was not excessive. The transaction duly occurred and the painting then hung on the wall at the New Zealand Residence for several years, before its return to New Zealand in the 1980s for restoration.

The all-consuming task of Britain's European ambitions impinged on our private life in Brussels, but by far the most compelling distraction during our time there was the birth of our first two children – John and Georgia – in 1968 and 1972 at the Croix Rouge Hospital. It was the rule in Belgium that a child must be named within 24 hours of its birth. I recall on both occasions a well upholstered and starched Flemish matron standing with a clipboard in hand, at the foot of Elizabeth's bed, barking 'Name?' Belgium was moreover one of the world's leading beer producers and consumers. One birthtime idiosyncrasy was to serve new mothers with large glasses of a famous Belgian dark beer known as Trappiste. I was able to share the burden of disposing of this medication on visits to Elizabeth.

Parents were required as well to register speedily the children's birth at the local Births, Deaths and Marriages Office in the Brussels commune where we lived. It was a very busy place. Along the wall by the entrance sat a queue of elderly Belgian returned servicemen. As I completed the registration, the clerk shouted 'Witness!' and the occupant at the head of the returned servicemen's queue approached the desk of the clerk, who then murmured '40 francs would be appropriate'. This was equivalent to a couple of New Zealand dollars, and I duly offered it to my witness. Following performance of his role, he then returned to the end of the queue to await his turn for another call to duty. In this way the seated returned servicemen daily discharged the same sequence of communal responsibility.

Brussels is a small city by European standards, and Belgium a small country, about the same size as Canterbury Province. A car journey of more than two hours terminates either at the border of a foreign country (Germany, Netherlands, Luxembourg or France) or the sea. Belgium, in its present and earlier geographical forms, has provided the battleground for much European conflict: Waterloo lies on the Brussels outskirts, and the Duke of Malborough fought two of his four famous victories on Belgian soil. But most graphically, in the First and Second World Wars of the 20th century widespread fighting occurred in and around Flanders and the large Ardennes forest in the east of the country. Many New Zealand soldiers from the First World War lie buried in the Belgian countryside.

Likewise, historically Belgium is a European centre of art and culture, with the towns of Bruges, Ghent and Antwerp, among others, possessing outstanding examples. The point here is that such landmarks are readily accessible to the residents of Brussels, and the O'Brien family were eventually served a double dose by virtue of the fact that a further and unanticipated posting back to Brussels awaited me. That repeat plunge into the shifting sands of New Zealand relations with the enlarged European Community was immediately preceded by immersion at Geneva, the supposed centre for international trade bargaining, where European agricultural protectionist instincts (and equivalent American inconstancy) ruled the roost. That common front had defeated all efforts in Geneva aimed at liberalising international agricultural trade.

Diplomatic life can be described as an exercise in interrupted destiny. One challenge any Ministry of Foreign Affairs confronts is to balance versatility with specialisation amongst its diplomats. It was a test of versatility, I supposed, that my immersion in the quicksands of New Zealand–European relations was immediately followed by successive diversions into the property and aid portfolios of External Affairs.

4. NEAR ABROAD

My participation in the Bernie Galvin aid expedition to the Cook Islands in 1975 meant that it was not a complete surprise that I was shoulder tapped shortly thereafter for a posting to Rarotonga. I was to be the first Head of Mission appointed by External Affairs to a post previously administered by the Department of Island Territories, which the new Kirk Government had disbanded earlier in the 1970s. I was in effect to be New Zealand's first diplomatic representative to a small country of fellow New Zealand citizens – which was something of a riddle in itself.

The physical beauty and admirable climate of Rarotonga, the main island and the capital, strikes you right from the outset. The New Zealand Residence, Ngatipa, was set on an elevated slope and blessed with a wonderful garden containing many coloured bougainvillea, tamarind, jacaranda, mango and Indian flame trees planted by the first British-appointed representative in the 19th century, as well as avocado trees that produced fruit the size of a small rugby ball.

The original 19th century wooden house had been replaced (courtesy of the New Zealand Ministry of Works) with a white-painted concrete-block home in the form of three pavilions joined by walkways across attractive lily ponds stocked with goldfish. The blemishes of modern tourism had not touched Rarotonga to the extent they have today. Indeed the Ministry of Works-built Ngatipa had been conceived as motel-style accommodation for visiting New Zealand public servants, as well as providing accommodation for the New Zealand Resident Commissioner. It was not therefore really a family home as such (it had concrete floors, eight bedrooms and numerous bathrooms), although its lovely setting, attractive exterior and the fact that Rarotonga's admirable climate encouraged much outside living were definite compensations.

Ngatipa possessed other features. There was one bedroom that sported a brass plate over the door saying 'Queen Elizabeth Slept Here', which she had when visiting Rarotonga in January 1974 to formally open the island's airport. Our youngest son Daniel occupied that room. There was amusing correspondence on office files concerning my predecessor's recommendations to Wellington for extra budget funds to install a silent flush toilet for the en suite in the Queen's smallish room. This initially produced a flat refusal from the New Zealand Treasury. There were fevered cables back and forth before my predecessor, clearly frustrated at Wellington's beggarliness, ordered the installation at his own initiative literally on the eve of the Queen's arrival.

My idyllic first impression of a South Pacific paradise, where everything moved delightfully at its own pace, was soon belied by an animating encounter with Cook Islands politics. My appointment was meant to supply tangible proof that New Zealand intended its links with Rarotonga to move away from the old colonial relationship, and henceforth approximate to a more regular diplomatic and mature connexion that better reflected the Cooks' status as 'self governing in free association with New Zealand' – which incidentally allowed the Cooks the right to appoint their own head of state. My predecessors had worn two hats: head of state and New Zealand representative. Throughout my term, however, there was in fact only an acting head of state, in the person of the Chief Justice (the New Zealand judge Gaven Donne), because the Cook Islands Government of Sir Albert Henry was unable to rally sufficient votes in the small parliament to amend the constitution to allow it to appoint a Cook Islander to the post.

When I arrived, Sir Albert Henry had led the Cooks throughout the 12 years since the grant of 'self government in free association'. In the small setting his personality, intelligence and shrewdness were paramount. He sought also to cut a figure beyond the Cooks in the South Pacific Forum. A general election was scheduled for March 1978 and the question was whether Sir Albert, who was then 72 years old, would lead the country into and beyond that election. In private conversation he would frequently assert (in the time honoured way of political leaders just about anywhere) that he wished to step aside but that there was no suitable successor. Sir Albert could be very amusing and yet most infuriating, almost at one and the same moment, in our frequent encounters throughout my assignment.

The extent of the Henry influence was pervasive and variously resented in the Cooks, including amongst traditional chiefs on Rarotonga. Thanks to Sir Albert the family occupied several positions in Cooks' political life: Sir Albert's eldest son was Internal Affairs Minister (and controlled the radio, which was the Premier's prime communication tool with the distant outer islands); his second son, Head of Public Works; his cousin, Minister of Finance; his sister, Speaker of the House of Representatives; his youthful grandson, nominal head of the minuscule External Affairs Department. There were others beyond Rarotonga linked by marriage and kinship to the Henrys, including in neighbouring Tahiti.

My letter of appointment to the position of New Zealand Representative in Rarotonga, signed by Foreign Minister Brian Talboys, described the new task as 'a difficult responsibility' with a degree of contact with the host government 'not experienced at any other New Zealand mission overseas'. The New Zealand aim, the Minister wrote, was 'to build a more mature relationship with the Cook Islands by pushing out the limits of what self government can offer to both of us'. There was in other words, at the New Zealand end, a perceptible ingredient of trial and error in the whole exercise – and so it proved. Indeed one sign of the complexity was that this letter of ministerial guidance, which in the normal course is available to a new envoy right at the beginning of his or her appointment, only arrived after I had been on the island for 12 months.

For half a century or longer, throughout colonial times, the Cooks had been the object of multiple New Zealand social, cultural, anthropological and economic studies. These now gathered dust on shelves and were of limited relevance. There were sparse archival resources available about more recent times, which may have been the result of the extinction of the old Department of Island Territories. There was a gap too in continuity of the official New Zealand presence on Rarotonga. My predecessor had resigned abruptly many months earlier, at the time of the suppression of the Islands' Affairs Department. My knowledge of the Cooks and its history was minimal and I did not speak Cook Islands Māori. The extensive family connexions within the Cooks that helped explain much of what transpired (especially in relation to the Henry influence) had to be learnt on the job, but I never completely understood them.

It was important to remember that the ideas for constitutional change to the Cook Islands–New Zealand relationship originated from the New Zealand side, not from the Cooks. There had never been indigenous clamour by Cook Islanders for independence. In the era of decolonisation that followed World War II there was, however, a firm belief amongst External Affairs founding fathers in Wellington that New Zealand's broader interests and international standing would best be served by progressively divesting New Zealand of the South Pacific tutelage that it had exercised as supervisor in regard to Samoa, the Cook Islands, Niue and Tokelau. The best departmental legal minds were directed to devise a new constitutional foundation for the Cooks, which took the form of 'self governing in free association with New Zealand', one that inter alia allowed Cook Islanders to retain New Zealand citizenship, appoint their own head of state and run their own affairs, including their priorities for economic development.

There were moments during the taxing times ahead, when dealing with Sir Albert Henry's capricious management, that I devoutly wished that those in Wellington who had imaginatively conceived the new Cooks' status had themselves been obliged to implement their elegant constitutional design on the spot. The role of lawyers is indispensable, of course, to the international relations of conscientious democracies like New Zealand, but in the face of the inescapable political complexity involved with those relations everywhere, the contribution by lawyers is not necessarily always sufficient or plausible. None of the External Affairs founding fathers had themselves actually served in the South Pacific. Over the two generations covered in this volume, it is interesting as well that of the ten heads of the Ministry since its foundation, only two have served in the South Pacific.

I came to question whether the model of Westminster-style adversarial politics bequeathed by New Zealand was actually fit for purpose in the pocket-handkerchief setting of Rarotonga, where the pool of talent was not wide or deep, at least in the Albert Henry era. It split the community and certainly deepened animosities between families and factions in ways that complicated the goal of greater self reliance within the Cooks. It took me a while to realise, for example, that the receptions we held at Ngatipa, which were frequent and sometimes quite boozy, provided virtually the sole occasions where political opponents actually mixed and socialised one with another. It must be admitted that after refreshment had been taken, there were occasional adversarial moments. At our farewell party the MP for the local village, Tupapa, landed a perfect right hook on the opposition candidate (a general election was imminent) sending him sprawling into one of Ngatipa's goldfish ponds.

As colonial supervisor for over 60 years, New Zealand had concentrated upon reproducing in the Cooks the sort of society that we sought for New Zealand itself – with particular emphasis on individual social welfare. Any systematic plans for productive economic development in the Cooks took second place to social wellbeing (in health, education, etc.). In the process some Cook Islands traditions and customs were compromised, while New Zealand's benevolence introduced lifestyle expectations that exceeded those in some other South Pacific countries (or even parts of New Zealand itself) and exceeded Cooks' capacities alone to fund. Rebalancing the New Zealand aid package to emphasise greater economic self reliance in the Cook Islands, which was implicit in 'self government in free association', was clearly to be an uphill task.

One responsibility of the New Zealand Representative's Office, as indeed of other New Zealand missions in the South Pacific at the time, was to encourage newly emergent Pacific Islands governments to widen their external relationships and therefore their access to additional sources of external assistance. New Zealand pockets were not deep enough to bear all the costs of economic and social development needed to reflect political change throughout the region. This is worth recalling at the time of this present writing, when New Zealand anxieties are aroused by the interest and activity of China in the region. New Zealand needs always to tread prudently lest it appear to be 'choosing friends' for the South Pacific, after having actively encouraged the region to seek out new partners.

Constraints upon the Cook Islands' economic progress included minute scale, dispersion through 15 widely scattered islands, absence of mineral resources, and a traditional system of land tenure (particularly on Rarotonga) that diminished productivity, plus the benefit of shared citizenship, which allowed and perhaps encouraged a brain drain of Cook Islanders to New Zealand. As New Zealand aid increasingly targeted productivity in the Cooks' agriculture sector, the levels of agricultural production, and the population, were steadily declining.

That became a topic of periodic hearty conversations with the Premier and his ministers.

The situation of the Minister of Agriculture captured the predicament neatly. He was a principal shareholder in Rarotonga's only supermarket, where, courtesy of Air New Zealand, air-freighted New Zealand fresh vegetables, fruit and fish were available at inflated prices. At the same time, as Agriculture Minister with New Zealand aid support, he was committed to increasing domestic production of many of the self-same products, which flourished readily in the Cook Islands and the surrounding seas. Abandoned citrus orchards on Rarotonga, whose climate is particularly conducive to citrus production, were sober evidence of the wider problem.

When New Zealand demurred at aid requests on grounds of project feasibility and/or competing priorities for available New Zealand funds, the political temperature could rise. One combustible example was the 1976 visit by a team from Wellington, led by Ray Jermyn, to review the aid programme and chart forward projects with the Cooks' authorities. At first things proceeded smoothly, but the visit ended on the final day in the Cabinet room with thunderous rebukes, table thumping and door slamming as Sir Albert walked out, all because the team indicated that New Zealand aid could not fund a vote-catching water reticulation project adjacent to Sir Albert's home village.

Ray Jermyn, an easy-going individual, was visibly mortified, and at the airport later that day as he prepared to leave, he duly recorded his dismay and exasperation. At that time the Cooks Government required passengers to fill in an airport departure card with two questions: 'How much money did you bring into the Cooks?' and 'How much money are you taking out of the Cooks upon departure?' Ray entered '$6 million' (which was the annual New Zealand aid budget for that year) in answer to the first question, and then '$6 million' again in answer to the second question. He returned his card at the gate, and hurried for his plane.

On the opposite side of the same coin there were undeniable New Zealand shortcomings – legacies of earlier times. New Zealand departments and business people with an established place (and interests) in the Cooks found adjustments to the new 'self governing in free association' relationship to be something of a trial. The New Zealand Representative's Office found itself arguing the Cooks' corner with Wellington in several respects: unanticipated increased air and shipping freight rates to New Zealand; the monopoly of air landing rights and Air New Zealand's inconsiderate scheduling of its flights; and the absence of any agricultural extension activity from the Totokoitu Research Station, which was established on Rarotonga and run by the New Zealand Department of Scientific and Industrial Research with no effective Cooks' input or apparent direct benefit.

The New Zealand Office was also obliged to pursue forlorn causes. Even though its climate was highly conducive to citrus production, during my tenure Greggs of Dunedin decided to close down their juice cannery on Rarotonga and cease operations. This was a big blow: citrus and pineapple, along with copra, were the biggest potential export earners for the Cooks. The Office was instructed to try to avert the worst – even New Zealand Prime Minister Rob Muldoon got in on the act – but discussions with visiting Greggs owners proved futile. One could not argue with the facts. The cannery was programmed to take up to 600,000 cases of citrus, but total production was only 120,000 cases, and the same sizeable discrepancy applied to pineapple production.

Amidst the tribulations over New Zealand aid there were accomplishments. A key example at the time was the construction by the New Zealand Defence Force of airstrips in the southern Cooks group (Mangaia, Ma'uke, Mitiaro and Atiu). Elizabeth and I flew in small Britten-Norman Islander aircraft to visit these new facilities, a journey that had taken my predecessors a matter of weeks by boat. Amongst the northern Cooks group only Penrhyn, near the equator, sported an airstrip, built by the Americans in World War II. A round trip to Penrhyn by boat took even longer than travelling to the southern Cooks. Its only air link was spasmodically supplied by New Zealand Ministry of Transport calibration flights, which offered an intermittent four-hour link to the island (allowing the New Zealand office to visit), and usually made the return flight to Rarotonga laden with handicrafts and the like for sale to tourists – who of course never got as far as Penrhyn.

ɷ

It is a venerable law of journalism of course that bad news invariably attracts publicity. Alleged wrongdoings about aid misappropriation on Rarotonga, and Sir Albert's periodic public outbursts about New

Zealand 'interference', featured often in New Zealand media. Things reached a new high, however, with the arrival on the island in early 1977 of Milan Brych, a professed Czech cancer therapist who had acquired popular renown in New Zealand for his work at Auckland Hospital. He had indeed been the subject of a laudatory New Zealand television documentary and had been voted in second place (after Prime Minister Norman Kirk) in the 1974 'Kiwi of the Year' poll.

However, parts of the New Zealand medical community were suspicious of Brych's methods and claims. After extensive examination by Auckland Hospital's Medical Advisory Committee, which had involved investigations undertaken by New Zealand specialists in Czechoslovakia itself, Brych had been declared a fraud. There had been extensive publicity and he had unsuccessfully resorted to the Wellington Court of Appeal.

It was not clear at the New Zealand Representative's Office just where the idea to invite Brych to set up shop in Rarotonga actually originated. Sir Albert was almost certainly involved but the project may have first been pushed by one or more of of his ministers. Be that as it may, problems immediately surfaced. Brych was allocated one ward, at least, for his patients at the Rarotonga Hospital – the centrepiece of New Zealand aid to the Cooks' health sector. The New Zealand medical authorities were appalled that a practitioner dismissed by them as a fraud should be allowed to now avail himself of and profit from New Zealand-supported health aid facilities in this way. They quickly forbade any referrals by New Zealand doctors to the new Brych clinic on Rarotonga, and the New Zealand Health Department discontinued a regular blood supply programme. This had the effect of extending the 'politics' of the Brych saga coincidentally into Australia. There was no referral ban by Australian health authorities, so from April 1977 the bulk of the cancer patients who began arriving on Rarotonga were Australian. Brych's activities then became a hot potato for Australia and its media. A constant reminder of his presence on the island was the frequent sight of his patients in the street, and more vividly, the appearance of a new cemetery opposite the airport, where those who had not responded successfully to his treatment lay buried. All of this lent grimness to the sunny beauty of Rarotonga.

A second figure who cast influence over Rarotonga was the American stamp millionaire Finbar Kenny, prominent in the philatelic world and contracted to many governments (including the Vatican) for stamp design and distribution services. His visits by private Lear jet to Rarotonga, and the parties he threw on the island, guaranteed a full turnout of Cooks' cabinet ministers, readily exceeding the numbers assembled to greet any New Zealand minister. Sir Albert had first met Kenny while attending the United Nations in 1965 in New York. He entered into an agreement, involving some due diligence by Wellington, to design and market Cook Islands' stamps, with the proceeds being split. All costs were to be borne by Kenny.

The persistent underlying political question on tiny Rarotonga was what happens when Sir Albert departs, and who will be his successor? Sir Albert's opponents united, more or less, around the figure of Dr Tom Davis, in the so-called Democratic Party. It was said that in their younger days relations between the two personalities had been amicable, but animosity now ruled in the small hothouse of Cooks politics. Davis was not a natural politician but he was a man of accomplishment: the first qualified Cooks doctor trained at Otago University, and later Medical Officer on Rarotonga; a long-distance sailor navigating his yacht between New Zealand and the United States; and a specialist working on space medicine with NASA, the American space authority. While in the United States he had been called as an expert witness to testify at the official 1969 enquiry into the Massachusetts car accident at Chappaquiddick which killed a young woman and implicated Teddy Kennedy, the youngest of the famed Kennedy brothers – he could readily be imposed upon to recount the event. Davis's experience and urbanity meant he was a personality around which political opposition to Sir Albert could rally.

The political implications of Finbar Kenny's interest in the Cooks came into fuller focus in the months before the March 1978 election, scheduled by Sir Albert. The electoral campaign had already made crystal clear that the result would be close. Tensions ran high and intrigue rampant. Cook Islanders resident in New Zealand (whose numbers at least equalled those residing in the Cooks) could only vote by casting their ballot in the Cook Islands. Unbeknown to the New Zealand Representative's Office and others, a plot was hatching between Sir Albert and Kenny whereby the latter would advance to the Premier and his political party a sum of money representing the estimated returns on future profits one year in advance. This would be used to charter passenger aircraft (Ansett Airways) to fly in voters from New Zealand, paying nominal fares ($20 each) and generously fed and watered, to cast their ballots at a voting booth especially set up at the airport and then immediately fly the return trip. The opposition party, the Democrats, had a similar plan in mind, but passengers on their charters (Air Nauru) paid the full fare, or something like it.

The 30 March election result conferred a two-thirds majority victory upon Sir Albert's party. This was immediately and unsurprisingly challenged by the Democratic Party on the grounds of electoral bribery. My assignment ended on the eve of the election itself, so the intricate legal battles and political duplicity which ensued provided an immediate burden for my able successor, Brian Absolum. Suffice to recall here that finally, in July 1978, the Cooks' Chief Justice and acting Head of State Gaven Donne declared the whole process to be illegal. He did not, however, order a fresh election; instead, after sifting through the poll results in each individual electorate, he declared the opposition party candidates in the majority of those electorates to be rightfully elected – thus bestowing on Tom Davis's Democratic Party a parliamentary majority. The judgement in effect unseated an 'elected' government and installed the opposition; it was, I believe, a first amongst established democracies anywhere. Meanwhile Finbar Kenny was pursued by US authorities for contravening American law.

It was clear well in advance that, depending on the election outcome, Milan Brych's days on Rarotonga were numbered. Davis had made it plain that were he and his party ever to be in government, he would denounce Brych's registration in the Cooks. Following hard on the heels of the bizarre election outcome, the Brych clinic on Rarotonga therefore folded and the man himself departed for the US, where he eventually fell foul of American law and suffered the consequences. The tortuous connections between Brych, Kenny and the Cooks Government is captured in the book *Milan Brych: The Cancer Man*, by the Australian journalist Frank Quill, which is not totally unsympathetic to Brych, nor indeed to Sir Albert.

The Premier did not himself escape strict official censure. His knighthood, bestowed personally by the Queen, was revoked. This was a harsh penalty, all things considered; around that time the same retribution was being meted out in the UK to the Soviet spy Sir Anthony Blunt, on the grounds of treason, and Sir Albert's misdeeds were hardly in that league. Moreover others, including New Zealanders, have been known to retain identical awards, despite impropriety.

ೲ

Three particular New Zealand official visits to Rarotonga during my term provided a trifecta. The first, in August 1976, was by the New Zealand Governor-General Sir Denis Blundell. It is an established rite of passage for New Zealand Governors-General to visit the Cooks. In the months prior to Sir Denis's call, the Premier had failed for a third time to secure the required two-thirds majority for passage of a bill that would allow the Cooks to appoint their own head of state; so when Sir Denis arrived, head of state responsibilities in the Cooks were being exercised in an acting capacity by Chief Justice Gaven Donne.

I had been on Rarotonga just six months. When Sir Denis arrived with wife, daughter and an aide-de-camp, to whom we extended board and lodging, I recounted to him the Premier's setback and emphasised the delicacy of any talk about full Cook Islands independence. It was therefore perplexing when the very next day, during his inaugural formal address in full vice-regal rig to assembled worthies and the Cooks Government (also broadcast over radio to the outer islands), Sir Denis dwelt purposefully upon New Zealand's responsibility to lead the Cook Islands along the road to full independence.

At that stage I had nothing in writing by way of official guidance about New Zealand's broader long-term objectives in regard to the Cooks. I was aware that there was an element of trial and error in the relationship we were now trying to establish, although this had not been confirmed to me in writing. But upon hearing Sir Denis's lucid assertion my first reaction was to question whether I was on the same wavelength as Wellington – after all, Sir Denis had presumably been briefed before his departure from New Zealand. In reporting subsequently to Wellington about the visit, I highlighted the apparent discrepancy.

The actual Blundell visit had its moments. Sir Albert was determined to demonstrate that he and his government were in charge and that the acting head of state was a secondary figure. There was much actual physical jostling and elbowing at official events to ensure Sir Albert's primacy alongside Sir Denis, some of it quite amusing. As I was preparing for the formal airport arrival of the vice-regal party, a harrowed Gaven Donne telephoned at the eleventh hour to request a lift to the airport, as his official car had been suddenly sequestered by the politicians for their purposes. Another memorable moment was when Rarotonga suffered a total electricity blackout in the middle of the dinner offered to Sir Denis and party at Ngatipa. We scrambled to find candles, which actually created a pleasing spectacle on a balmy Rarotonga evening, with bougainvillea flowers decorating the rooms and verandah. The food cooking in the kitchen ovens was ruined, however. Such was life.

In January 1977 the Rt Hon. Brian Talboys, the first ever New Zealand Foreign Minister to visit the Cook Islands, arrived in Rarotonga, accompanied by the Deputy Secretary of Foreign Affairs, Merv Norrish. We offered board and lodging. This was an event conceived (on the New Zealand side anyway) to symbolise the new maturity in the relationship between the Cooks and New Zealand. It was a first exposure for the Cooks to senior political level conduct of New Zealand foreign policy. In the lead up to the visit Sir Albert had contrived public statements which criticised New Zealand 'interference' in the Cooks through the aid programme. That was not a helpful omen.

During official talks, Talboys confirmed the strategy behind an increased aid package: in consultation with Cook Islands authorities, New Zealand would energise the productive sectors of the Cooks' economy (agriculture, etc.) while reducing support for social and budgetary expenditure, which would increasingly become the responsibility of the Cook Islands Government. During the visit it became clear Sir Albert himself was quite aware of the implications behind the new New Zealand aid package – namely that hard and sensitive choices between competing economic and social priorities were now inevitable for his government. Sir Albert's resulting political shenanigans did not impress the New Zealand Foreign Minister. Moreover the political temperature of New Zealand–Cooks relations was infused by the Brych affair. Talboys felt it necessary to place squarely on the record, by letter, that the whole business was unacceptable to New Zealand. He responded as well through the media, repudiating Sir Albert's continued claims of New Zealand interference that had incidentally targeted the New Zealand Representative's Office for particular castigation.

Reflecting on the visit afterwards, it was edifying that senior levels from Wellington had been exposed first hand to the reality of Cook Islands politics under Sir Albert, and therefore to the everyday challenges confronted by the New Zealand Office in Rarotonga. There is always uncertainty at overseas diplomatic missions lest their reporting of problems to head office is considered excessive. At least this ministerial visit should have helped dispel any concerns on that score.

The third memorable event was the visit to Rarotonga in May 1977 by Prime Minister Rob Muldoon, who was on his way to the Commonwealth Prime Ministers Conference in Gleneagles, Scotland, at which the vexatious issue of sporting contacts with apartheid South Africa was to figure prominently. We were generally aware in the New Zealand Office that relations between the Prime Minister and Minister of Foreign Affairs were, as a result, somewhat prickly. The New Zealand Representative's Office was instructed that the PM did not want to overcharge the programme in the Cooks (no outer islands visits, etc.), which in the circumstances was entirely reasonable. His chief task anyway was to participate at the official opening of the new Rarotonga Hotel, in which Air New Zealand and the New Zealand Tourism Department had made substantial investment. He arrived on a charter flight with Mrs Muldoon and 127 fellow New Zealand invitees to the opening festivities, which included the Secretaries of Foreign Affairs, Transport and the Treasury, as well as others, all with spouses. Sir Albert grumbled to me privately beforehand that he hoped there would be sufficient room for Cook Islands guests at the opening ceremony.

The gala opening was notable for traditional Cook Islands entertainment. The claim that the Cooks possess the best dancers and drummers in the South Pacific is not an idle one. The abundant decorations bore testament as well to the talent and exquisite eye which Cook Islanders possess. The Prime Minister himself was even prevailed upon to dance Cook Islands-style with Elizabeth (she later took care to ensure a photographic record was disappeared). But it was not all sweetness and light. As the various guests assembled in the hotel reception area to be greeted by the hosts, Sir Albert pulled a typical rabbit from his hat by extracting from the throng the controversial self-proclaimed cancer therapist Milan Brych for presentation to the Prime Minister and Mrs Muldoon. The PM, taking it in his stride, peremptorily acknowledged the errant medicine man. It was my only physical contact with the individual who, after barely three months on the island, was proving such a bane to New Zealand–Cooks relations.

At his collective meeting with the Cook Islands Cabinet two days later, the PM outlined quietly but firmly the political problems which the Brych activities on Rarotonga were causing government in New Zealand. He carefully avoided any direct accusation of Cooks' wrongdoing but was crystal clear about New Zealand's opposition to the whole business and went out of his way to express openly the government's firm support for the role of the New Zealand Representative's Office (bearing in mind Sir Albert's periodic charges of interference). During his stay on the island I noticed the PM was careful never once to disparage Sir Albert or the Cooks' Government privately to me – as some other high-ranking New Zealand visitors felt free to do.

A flash of acerbic prime ministerial humour illuminated Muldoon's last full day. The afternoon had been left free for a fishing trip around Rarotonga and the Prime Minister's immediate party duly assembled on the wharf at Avatiu Harbour. It was a beautiful day and the small attractive wooden-hulled fishing boat, with Minister of Internal Affairs Tupui Henry (Sir Albert's eldest son) as host, set out on a four-hour expedition.

The Cooks' hosts provided food and refreshment, which included delicious young coconuts into which the liquor of your choice (vodka, rum, gin, etc.) was poured to mix with the clear coconut milk. When finished, the empty husk was disposed of over the side of the boat, and a new young nut prepared. It was all very congenial out on the blue water, except that the fish declined to bite on any of the four long trailing lines behind the boat that were intended to catch marlin, tuna or whatever.

After nearly four hours at sea, the skipper announced it was time to turn back to harbour. Just then the lookout, a small boy at the mast, cried out 'Shark! Shark!' and sure enough we sighted dorsal fins cutting the water near our lines. The skipper shouted for more fish bait to be cast overboard to entice the sharks. The boy shouted back that we were out of bait – the buckets were empty.

At this moment the Prime Minister rose from his seat, having already cast a few coconut husks overboard, and in a voice heard by almost everybody declaimed 'Out of bait? Throw in the foreign affairs representatives!' After a pause which would have done credit to the most professional stand-up comedian, he then added, 'On second thoughts, foreign affairs representatives are an acquired taste – even for sharks.' These remarks were greeted with much mirth, except by the serious-minded foreign affairs officer travelling in his party from Wellington, whose subsequent career was illustrious, but who remained woodenly impassive in the face of the PM's humour. As the boat neared the wharf the skipper reached into the cool hatch and retrieved a string of reef fish, which he handed to Muldoon to carry with him down the small gangplank to where a small crowd of Rarotongan onlookers awaited to see the New Zealand leader disembark after a successful day's fishing.

CR

I was a little bit wiser by the end of the Rarotonga assignment. Dealing with Sir Albert Henry had been stimulating, if sometimes deeply frustrating. There had been some stirring encounters over different issues at different times. The Premier was often very humorous. A sure sign of a broadside in the making was his habit of cracking his finger joints before expressions of reproach. Sir Albert had that uncanny ability to express himself at different levels with different meanings. It was always necessary after an encounter to sit and ponder carefully what the Premier had really been saying, as distinct from what he had actually said.

    There were real consolations aside from the beauty of Rarotonga and the warmth of its people. Our fourth child Tim was born at Rarotonga Hospital. His mother dispensed with the practice, favoured by almost all Kiwi expatriate mothers-to-be, of returning to New Zealand for the birth. That earned Elizabeth respect in the community. Margaret Makea Karika Ariki, Rarotonga's leading ariki, asked to be Tim's godmother and bestowed upon him a Cook Islands Māori second name – Tekao, meaning 'green shoot' and 'hope of the family'. It was a generous gesture at the end of an animating and at times entrancing two-year adventure in the Cooks.

5. TOUCHING BASE

Swerving from one responsibility to the next, and then back again, persisted after my South Pacific experience. I returned to Wellington once again, to the Ministry's Economic Division, this time as director with a team of first-rate young officers – Simon Murdoch, Maarten Wevers, Dick Grant – all destined for greater heights. Once again it proved abbreviated destiny. My role lasted barely two years from 1978 when another overseas excursion was decreed.

At the time three main issues lay at the Division's table, each with their own drama – fisheries, international aviation and multilateral trade liberalisation. Prolonged international negotiation of a newly minted Law of the Sea (LOS) had recently concluded, under which New Zealand acquired a maritime Exclusive Economic Zone (EEZ) extending sole rights over natural resources in the fourth largest marine area in the world. This represented a supreme 20th century diplomatic accomplishment for New Zealand, which owed everything to the skills of Malcolm Templeton, who led MFA and its lawyers to the outcome.

The New Zealand EEZ formally entered into force on 1 April 1977, and need therefore arose to negotiate a total allowable catch (TAC) with those deep-sea fishing nations that had traditionally fished New Zealand waters. The annual TAC was based upon estimated stocks in the zone that were surplus to the requirements of the New Zealand fishing industry. The actual extent of stocks was uncertain, but the governments of Japan, South Korea and the Soviet Union were waiting in line for negotiations with New Zealand, and the Ministry's Economic Division, under the overall supervision of Assistant Secretary Ian Stewart, was the 'go to' unit charged with carriage of those negotiations. This required close coordination, of course, with the responsible New Zealand fishery authorities, while the New Zealand fishing industry was itself seeking private joint ventures with overseas commercial fishing interests – there were some 30-odd proposals in the wind.

Differing opinions emerged, both inside MFA and at the political level in Wellington, about the extra negotiating clout that New Zealand had actually acquired through the LOS. Some believed the new rights now added appreciably to New Zealand's muscle, providing bargaining chips when it came to trade access negotiations, in particular with Japan. Amongst the small number of Japan specialists in MFA and inside New Zealand's Tokyo Embassy, however, there was no consensus about the extra leverage New Zealand now enjoyed.

But at the highest political level there was no agnosticism. Prime Minister Rob Muldoon clearly believed New Zealand leverage was definitely enhanced, and moreover that he understood Japanese negotiating culture. He decided a forthright message was called for, which he intended to deliver personally. Japan's fish quota and access entitlement would, in his mind, depend squarely on Japanese removal of trade restrictions upon New Zealand agricultural exports.

Following a meeting with the Japanese Minister of Agriculture and Fisheries in a hotel room in Melbourne (the PM was primarily in Melbourne to attend the 1978 funeral of Sir Robert Menzies), where it seems there was actually no one else present, Muldoon announced publicly that he had indeed reached an understanding that a 'fish for beef' deal (as the media christened it) with Japan was on the cards. Whether the Japanese shared this view about the outcome of the meeting was not clear. The Prime Minister then added to this conviction with a widely reported speech castigating Japanese 'economic imperialism'. This provided the overture for the actual imminent fisheries negotiations.

They opened in a blaze of TV camera lights at Parliament Buildings, with Ian Stewart leading the New Zealand delegation. It was quickly clear the large Japanese delegation sought to confine the agenda to the text of a fisheries agreement setting an actual Japanese catch quota – nothing else. The New Zealand side made it clear that the catch quota was a matter for New Zealand alone to decide on the basis of a finally negotiated fisheries agreement about access. Negotiation proceeded on this basis over the weeks ahead until texts were agreed for initialling by the delegations. The New Zealand text was referred to the Cabinet. At this point, on cue, the PM intervened publicly and pungently through the media. He dismissed the 'diplomatic language' of the draft agreement and called for greater 'clarification'.

The Japanese were mortified. Joint signature was delayed. The situation of Japanese fishing vessels actually inside the New Zealand zone at the time was threatened. A period of posturing, shadow-boxing and delay then ensued at the New Zealand political level before finality was reached. There was no substantive change to the outcome skilfully negotiated by Ian Stewart; and there was no agreement or understanding linking fisheries access and trade. Bulldozing had not worked.

The Russians tried a different ploy and sent Fisheries Minister Aleksandr Ishkov to negotiate an agreement with New Zealand. He was a canny, durable individual, first appointed People's Commissar for Fisheries in 1939 and thus somehow a survivor of the disappearances and bloodletting purges of the grim Stalin era. He arrived in Wellington in 1978 and immediately proved more forthcoming about notions of 'fish for trade'. On the margins of the actual negotiations, he suggested five-year access to the Soviet market for New Zealand dairy and meat exports in return for a guaranteed five-year Soviet TAC in New Zealand's EEZ, which would involve a joint venture with New Zealand fishing interests. New Zealand's insistence that catch quotas were for New Zealand alone to decide, on top of political hesitations, ruled out that enticement.

Ishkov travelled the North Island. I accompanied him. In Rotorua a highly convivial evening with local MP and former Minister of Tourism Harry Lapwood produced a night of musical and cultural contrast. Ishkov, with a reputation as a fine trained singer, was imposed upon to demonstrate his talent to the assembled diners, which he did impressively in deep bass tones with his delegation supplying gentle back-up. Lapwood, a large imposing figure who had served as Regimental Sergeant Major with the New Zealand Division in Greece and Crete, was then prevailed upon to reply in kind. He led proceedings with seven excruciatingly hearty verses of 'Old MacDonald's Farm', complete with a whole repertoire of animal noises, supported by his delegation in spirited unison. What the Russians made of the depth and width of the cultural divide on display was anyone's guess.

The international politics of civil aviation disclosed protectionist instincts at this time inside senior levels at Air New Zealand. They were aroused particularly by US President Jimmy Carter's crusade for global agreement on an 'open skies' policy, which would permit unrestricted airline services to, from and beyond all territories of the countries involved, without prescribing where carriers flew, the number of flights operated, or the prices charged. Such a dose of free market medicine was resisted stoutly by New Zealand's national carrier, but inside MFA, after due deliberation, there was consensus that New Zealand should pursue the idea further, and accede to a US request for official-level consultations. These were eventually set for March 1979.

The formidable Air New Zealand Chief Executive Morrie Davis positioned himself unexpectedly in the wings of these Washington consultations, where I was involved. He forthrightly warned a huddle of the New Zealand delegation members beforehand that 'heads would roll' in Wellington if MFA pushed for New Zealand to embrace the Carter policy. Even though he was strictly 'outside the room' of the negotiations proper, the force of Davis's gimlet-eyed personality clearly held sway over the Secretary of the New Zealand Ministry of Transport and Civil Aviation, who led the New Zealand side. Middle-level policy officers of that Ministry informally encouraged MFA, however, to keep pressing 'open skies'.

Likewise, in respect to Japan – where MFA had been disposed to explore civil aviation cooperation, including landing rights, as one means to broaden the New Zealand–Japan relationship – the Ministry was told that Air New Zealand was not interested in landing rights in Tokyo. Britain, too, formally requested aviation discussions to allow their designated carrier (British Airways) two extra flights per week into New Zealand, in return for granting Air New Zealand reciprocal rights into London. The MFA collective view was that there were good foreign policy reasons for considering the British request. Air New Zealand again informed MFA they were simply not interested.

These days, when tourism is New Zealand's number one foreign exchange earner and Air New Zealand established as a rewarding, progressive international airline, all of this sounds eccentric. The ambiguity which coloured the picture of broadening New Zealand civil aviation policy at the time was part of the wider protectionist sentiment across the New Zealand economy.

Protectionism also inhabited the more familiar ground of international trade and New Zealand's commitment to secure greater liberalisation for agriculture. The so-called Tokyo Round of multilateral trade liberalisation was, after six laborious years, coming to an end in the General Agreement on Tariffs and Trade (GATT) at Geneva in 1979. Once more, liberalisation of farm trade was effectively brushed aside. The major economies, especially the US and EEC, were not prepared for change.

New Zealand's position in the negotiations was itself ambivalent. Our negotiators in Geneva continued to insist, under instruction from the Department of Trade and Industry, that New Zealand's import licensing system was not up for negotiation, even as in the next breath they urged relaxation of protectionist policies upon others for agricultural trade. MFA sought to underscore this lack of consistency and its effect on New Zealand's credibility at coordination meetings in the Cabinet Economic Committee in Wellington. The Prime Minister, true to form, publicly and vehemently deplored the 'lunacy' of Europe's Common Agricultural Policy in ways calculated to ruffle feathers in Brussels, where the idea of introducing an EEC sheep meat regulation had reared its head.

Elsewhere trade policy, especially with regard to Australia, was in the wind of change. Fruitless discussion on extending the product coverage of the 1965 New Zealand–Australia Free Trade Agreement (NAFTA) persisted, but patience was ebbing. Attention was turning to a different approach – a closer overall economic relationship between the two countries. Foreign Minister Brian Talboys and Trade Minister Hugh Templeton had each begun testing the ground. In March 1980, Prime Ministers Rob Muldoon and Malcolm Fraser, though not the best of friends, jointly announced their commitment to pursuit of Closer Economic Relations (CER).

My experience at this time with covering a suite of contemporary external economic issues brought home the way in which personal satisfaction is disappointed by the very nature of the job, because the final curtain of closure rarely descends. The game of musical chairs inevitably involved in external relations work, whether at home or abroad, means that issues which consume attention while occupying a particular seat persist after that seat is vacated, as the three areas – fisheries, aviation and trade policy – I have described here amply illustrate. The job consists of stewardship more than a cut-and-dried, completed transaction. So it was that in late 1979, as Air New Zealand's protectionist battles were about to be grimly overshadowed by New Zealand's biggest aviation disaster – the tragic plane crash at Mount Erebus in Antarctica – I was readying for other pasture.

I was fortunate to be given the opportunity to participate in a six-week course devoted to international economic relations, courtesy of the US Government, at the Brookings Institution in Washington. This provided energising exposure to a whole range of opinion and knowledge from a raft of contributors (some of them quite distinguished) with expertise in international politics and economics, which proved useful in my next posting.

6. LAKESIDE

The next offshore posting, as Ambassador to Geneva, could hardly have been a greater contrast with my preceding overseas assignment in Rarotonga. Geneva, nestling at the southern end of its lake, surrounded by mountains on either side, presented a sublime appearance, summer and winter. It was clean, green, tidy, sophisticated and expensive in a distinctively Swiss way. Greater familiarity over time confirmed a formal and antiseptic quality to the city – a version of beauty lacking a soul. Geneva took itself seriously. The contrast with warm, casual and slightly zany Rarotonga was considerable.

For a New Zealand resident Geneva's size was quite manageable – the population when my family and I landed in early 1980 was about the same as Wellington. It provides the headquarters for multiple United Nations organisations and is populated with legions of international civil servants – employed in an alphabet soup of big agencies like the World Health Organization (WHO), the International Labour Organization (ILO), the World Intellectual Property Organization (WIPO), the World Meteorological Organization (WMO), the United Nations Conference on Trade and Development (UNCTAD), the United Nations Committee on Disarmament (UNCD), the United Nations Human Rights Committee, the High Commission for Refugees, and the General Agreement on Tariffs and Trade (GATT), which was later transfigured into the World Trade Organization (WTO).

There were in addition large non-governmental agencies like the International Red Cross, the World Council of Churches, and the World Wildlife Fund, as well as a host of smaller bodies. On top of all that was a veritable horde of diplomats, since many countries, unlike New Zealand at the time, accredited more than one ambassador to cover various agencies. The diplomats comprised a colony from which the Swiss people tended to keep their distance. They mingled with reserve.

The New Zealand residence was a pleasant, rented, mid-sized house in the village of Cologny, 20 minutes by car from the city, with a generous sloping garden of cherry and walnut trees looking out over Geneva and the lake with its famous fountain. It was a good place for entertaining. The village had been home to illustrious inhabitants like Mary Shelley, who wrote her famous book *Frankenstein* there whilst living in a threesome with her poet husband and Lord Byron in a villa 200 metres from the New Zealand residence. The house was family friendly, which was good because all four of our children accompanied us. All were enrolled at the Geneva International School, two in the English stream and two in the French stream. The children and parents of their classmates provided Elizabeth and I with the best chance to meet people with little connection to the all-consuming diplomatic throng. One schoolmate of our younger sons in Geneva was, for instance, the daughter of the chef at a local Michelin-starred restaurant, and her annual birthday party, which was held at the restaurant, included invitations to parents: a full house was guaranteed.

Work inside most Geneva agencies was concerned with improvement, one way or another, to global wellbeing – politically, economically, commercially and socially. The atmosphere at the time was affected by a sharpening polarisation between developed economies (the North) and developing economies (the South). In the US, the 1981 landslide election of President Reagan ushered in the ascendancy of neo-liberal supply-side economics (Reaganomics) for which Milton and Rose Friedman had written the gospel in 1980 with their book *Freedom to Choose*. This new 'religion' pervaded the work of many international agencies at Geneva. The New Zealand Mission got a foretaste when it hosted a US Senate Foreign Relations Committee delegation headed by the formidable isolationist senator Jesse Helms. In a slow, expressive southern drawl, Helms totally demolished the value and relevance of the United Nations and, particularly, the General Agreement on Tariffs and Trade.

Geneva's geographical situation served to illustrate how physical location conditions governments' ability to defend or advance interests. For Europeans Geneva is just a car ride, or comfortable train journey, or brief flight from their capitals. As a result, European influence over business at Geneva, especially on trade policy issues, overshadowed that of other participants, including even the US – which itself, of course, enjoys equivalent ascendancy over international economic and financial issues because the International Monetary Fund and the World Bank are situated in Washington. Whenever trade policy deliberations or negotiations got tough in Geneva, Europeans could promptly summon heavy cavalry from their home capitals and from Brussels. The competence of their officials was ubiquitous. In contrast, no country's cavalry has further to gallop to the negotiating haunts of Europe than New Zealand.

Trade policy and negotiation were a cardinal New Zealand priority in Geneva. But the duty of 'good global citizenship' and national interest spurred active involvements by the Mission in the other facets of Geneva activity. Indeed several of the issues (refugees, labour rights, human rights, health) had direct and sometimes sensitive domestic relevance inside New Zealand itself. The big annual conferences of WHO, ILO and GATT brought sizeable New Zealand delegations to Geneva which had to be serviced and entertained – the Cologny residence was a bonus in this last respect.

The need to coordinate and balance the New Zealand Mission's day-to-day involvements across the broad spectrum of Geneva responsibility was a test, but because New Zealand, unlike others such as Australia, had just one Ambassador covering the gamut of responsibilities, we avoided the silo effects of separate ambassadorial responsibilities, which compartmentalised issues that should have been connected.

At the time the Mission was, for instance, able to leverage involvements on trade policy issues inside the UNCTAD to secure a New Zealand presence at the inner councils of GATT, where major industrialised economies ruled the roost and where responsibility for actual trade negotiation lay. Making common cause with large developing countries in the United Nations body, against the pernicious agricultural protectionism practised by the major industrialised economies, led to those developing countries throwing support behind New Zealand involvement in the inner councils of GATT and the efforts there to liberalise farm trade. New Zealand's small share of total world trade would not have necessarily entitled it to a place in those inner councils otherwise.

A blow by blow account of New Zealand dealings with trade issues at Geneva nearly 40 years ago is pointless, but it is perhaps worth registering that there is nothing remarkable in the actual negotiation and intrigue involved with trade policy. An impression conveyed somewhat later, particularly by 'celebrity' New Zealand trade negotiators, sometimes implied a mystique surrounding the horse trading in Geneva and beyond, which the New Zealand person in the street could not possibly comprehend. That was an exaggeration.

A principal task for the Mission in my time was to generate support with others for preparation of yet another big round of collective negotiations to further liberalisation of international trade. Arthur Dunkel, a personable, capable Swiss who was the new Director-General at GATT, was energising the process. It was agreed the annual General Agreement Council be convened in 1982 at ministerial level (the last time this had been done was in 1973) to provide the necessary launch pad. Canada, by consensus, took the lead through its Deputy Prime Minister, Allan MacEachen, and its Geneva Ambassador, Don McPhail.

Severe wrangles soon emerged in the preparations about the priority areas for further liberalisation. New Zealand belonged, of course, in the camp which attached number one priority to agriculture (which was portrayed as 'unfinished business'). However, the major powers favoured priority to extending rules to newer areas of trade. When the moment duly arrived, sizeable ministerial delegations fronted at the 1982 meeting. New Zealand's seven-member delegation, led by Foreign Minister Warren Cooper with Deputy Trade Secretary Ted Woodfield from Wellington in the van, was more modest than many others.

The launch was decidedly eccentric. The Swiss Government threw a big party at the other end of Lake Geneva in the centuries old Château de Chillon (immortalised by Lord Byron), to which delegations were conveyed by special train. Around the battlements there were medieval strolling minstrels, serving wenches in low-cut blouses, and much toasting and quaffing. It was a distinctly odd theme for a 20th century trade negotiation. The negotiation quickly ran into appreciable difficulty, prompting the Canadian Chairman to add two extra days to proceedings. That meant several ministers and their home-based advisers (including New Zealand's) were actually obliged to depart before the end, leaving it to ambassadors to finish the deal in a bleary all night rumpus. They produced a Ministerial Declaration which was described by the Chair as 'stand against protectionism', but in terms of concrete results, let alone agreement to launch a new round of actual trade negotiations, it was pretty thin gruel.

From a New Zealand viewpoint the proceedings throughout were marked by sharp differences between the Canadian Chair and the Australian delegation, whose Trade Minister, Doug Anthony, made clear from the outset that Canberra was intent upon zeroing in on the European Community as the real villain in the piece, especially over agricultural trade liberalisation. MacEachen clearly found these tactics excessive and finally suspended the Australians from his small 'friends of the Chair' inner group (a traditional device in such major negotiations) and substituted New Zealand instead, with an instruction to 'keep the Australians informed'. This unforeseen rearrangement in New Zealand's favour provoked indignant Australian reactions that were audible to delegations on the conference floor.

The ministerial meeting did agree to establish a Committee for Agriculture under the General Agreement, for which the New Zealand Mission had lobbied hard, and which extended institutional recognition to agricultural trade that had been effectively denied by major powers for nearly 40 years. To herald the birth of yet another committee as a diplomatic triumph bears all the hallmarks of typical bureaucratic overhype. But the new body nonetheless provided a platform for successive New Zealand representatives in Geneva to play a role in a new round of multilateral trade liberalisation negotiations (christened the Uruguay Round) that was eventually agreed in 1986, after I had left the scene. Those negotiations were to last nine arduous years, and in 1995 transformed GATT into the World Trade Organization.

One responsibility assigned to the New Zealand Ambassador in Geneva was chairmanship of the International Dairy Products Council that had been established by the previous multilateral negotiations (the so-called Tokyo Round) that had ended in 1979, immediately prior to my arrival. The background to this is hardly worth recounting here but New Zealand clearly had an obvious prime interest in this new creation, and the Mission had lobbied hard to secure the chairmanship, which I assumed when I arrived.

Council membership was discretionary but it required signatory countries collectively to agree to and abide by minimum prices in the international market for key dairy products, and to engage in a regularised exchange of data about production, exports, and the like. Dairy-producing countries comprised the lion's share of the membership, which at its height stood at 14. The Council did bring together competing interests around one table for the first time. Essentially the aim was to curb downward pressures on world prices emanating from disposal of mountainous quantities of surplus European and American dairy products.

Non-government representation was not the practice, but the Mission was able to insert Dairy Board representation quietly into the Council room (Charles Patrick, whose skills and judgement served New Zealand's dairy interests throughout Europe). But ultimately the Europeans pushed for the Board's exclusion on the grounds it was leveraging involvement to undercut European sales; while the US eventually withdrew from the arrangement altogether on the grounds that the Dairy Board had colluded with the EEC, at America's expense, over sales to Russia and elsewhere. It was a double whammy, although neither claim was entirely unfounded. The arrangement limped on for 15 years, but with reduced integrity.

One other involvement warrants a brief note. I was approached to chair a three-person dispute panel between the US and Canada about whether Canadian rules on foreign investment were compatible with the rules of the General Agreement. The issue about foreign investment and trade rules was sensitive. It had been exercising important minds since the 1940s. I possessed no qualifications or expertise in the actual subject matter, but Wellington agreed I should assume the role. I was not 'representing' New Zealand as such. The role of 'holding the ring' in this way was a New Zealand first in Geneva. The two other panel members came from Japan and the Netherlands. Together with lawyers from the General Agreement's office, we cudgelled our brains over the subject matter.

This no place to recount the complexities and intricacies of the adjudication, which lasted several months. In broadest terms, the panel conclusions did not question Canadian foreign investment rules, but rather certain purchasing and export requirements therein, and

Canada undertook to abide by the findings. These were the days of ad hoc dispute arrangements, well before the formalised Appellate Court system set up by the WTO in 1995 (in which Chris Beeby of MFAT was to play a distinguished part). Trade lawyers and experts in North America, I later learnt, had a field day going through our panel's conclusions with a fine-tooth comb; and the findings also featured as a reference point during the 15-year negotiations for China's eventual WTO membership.

CR

Many of the lighter moments of my work in Geneva came from the lobbying of government delegations by groups with interests in the myriad issues concerning the Geneva institutions. A prime example involved the World Health Organization and its intention to adopt a new code on labelling of breastmilk substitutes at its 1981 Assembly. New Zealand was strongly in favour. The new Reagan administration in Washington, however, had made it clear that it would strenuously oppose all such regulation, and persuade others in the same direction, because the code interfered with liberal free-market orthodoxy.

NGO supporters of the code for their part mounted notable efforts, persuading hand-picked celebrities to lobby selected delegations in the corridors of the Assembly. The New Zealand delegation was targeted in the coffee shops at the conference site (the grand art-deco Palais des Nations) by Group Captain Peter Townsend, one-time candidate for the hand of the Queen's sister, Princess Margaret, together with Ingrid Thulin, a leading Swedish film actress and star of the acclaimed Ingmar Bergman film *Wild Strawberries*.

It was a model of organised persuasion. The crowning feature occurred on the morning of the vote itself, when the squads of dark-suited, briefcase-carrying male delegates scurrying up the steps of the UN headquarters found themselves obliged to navigate 50 or more unbuttoned mothers, with babies at the breast, ostentatiously standing their ground like line infantry across the entrance to the building. The impact of such heroics was palpable. The vote for the code an hour later was 118 in favour and one opposed (the US).

CR

There were other diversions. One such was the visit of Prime Minister Rob Muldoon to attend the Davos Economic Forum in 1982. This was one of the first annual Davos gatherings, which bring together the great and the good of the world at the small mountain ski resort in Switzerland. Muldoon's advocacy for international recognition of the critical connection between trade and finance, notably debt, had attracted international notice and led to his invitation to Davos. Basically he was arguing that the International Monetary Fund's exigent surveillance of debt-dependent economies had to be balanced by equivalent (symmetrical) surveillance of the policies (especially trade) of the lenders. Personally I felt the PM had a solid point. But some staff in the New Zealand Treasury and beyond had professional reservations about the implied criticism of IMF principles and practice.

A large dose of Murphy's Law attended the PM's participation at Davos. The Geneva Mission and the Embassy in Bonn (which was accredited to Switzerland) had received a somewhat peremptory message from the Prime Minister's Department stating there was no need for any assistance with the visit. The Davos organisers, we were told, had promised full care for the 'self contained' prime ministerial party, which was to arrive on the due date at Zurich, 120 kilometres from Davos. I had myself actually received a separate invitation from the organisers, who were based in Geneva. I had informed Wellington. I checked into a different Davos hotel from that selected for the PM and party.

In the event, the Davos organisers failed to show up at Zurich airport on the night of Muldoon's arrival. The PM and party had then become marooned for a long period in a sort of immigration no-man's-land after the private secretary (who was an old National Party brother-in-arms with little staff work experience) had cleared immigration and security, replete with all the party's passports and documentation, but was then firmly prevented from rejoining the PM and party by heavily armed Swiss police who were on sharp alert following a recent terrorist assault on Zurich airport. The Prime Minister was stranded.

It was after midnight, and snow was falling in Davos, when I was awakened at my hotel by a phone call from a member of the PM's party informing me of the mishap and warning the PM had been infuriated by the absence of the New Zealand Ambassador. When I gently remonstrated that we had been specifically informed by cable that no help was required, it became very clear from the caller's evasions that the PM himself had not actually been made aware of that message. It was one of those cases, not uncommon in the New Zealand public service, where dutiful subordinates, anxious to please a minister (particularly a demanding one), 'anticipate' the wishes of their master.

I wrote a quick note for Muldoon welcoming him and offering help should it be needed, although stating that I knew from prior cabled advice that his party was 'self sufficient'. I got dressed, and trudged through the midnight snow to deliver it at his hotel. That helped mend fences. He called by phone next morning and suggested a meeting. But more was to come. The PM was scheduled next day to be one of the first keynote speakers on a panel alongside German Chancellor Helmut Schmidt, French Finance Minister Raymond Barre, and the head of the World Bank, Tom Clausen. At the last moment the organisers had rescheduled some of the opening session and left messages at Muldoon's hotel to that effect, which the PM's tenderfoot secretary, unused to foreigners, their language and ways of expression, failed to absorb, let alone transmit.

I took the PM to the venue at due time, through the snow, to be greeted by the chief organiser with anguished demands as to why we were late. Proceedings had begun without the PM. In the event they were hurriedly adapted and Muldoon delivered his message. However the PM himself clearly found this persistence of Murphy's Law to be tedious, and declined to attend the gala black-tie dinner of Davos heavyweights on the final night. He was at a loose end. After paying a healthy black-market premium to a porter at the hotel, I managed to secure tickets for the sold-out final of the Swiss ice hockey championship being played at Davos that night, which the Prime Minister appeared to enjoy. I slipped away from Davos the next day.

At the end of three years in Geneva I was ready for a break. Both Elizabeth and I favoured a return home but, once again at short notice, I was cross-posted to my earlier stamping ground of Brussels. We were obliged to split the family in order to complete the children's school year in Geneva, so I rattled around alone in the Brussels accommodation for a couple of months while Elizabeth found lodgings in the Carouge suburb of Geneva. When the children completed the school year, she then drove the 800 kilometres to Brussels in the packed family car with four children and the pet rabbit. Such was life representing New Zealand.

7. BACK TO THE FUTURE

A repeat assignment to Brussels was not a duplicate of, nor an encore for, the experience ten years previously when Britain first gained entry into the European Community. Previous experience of course provided advantages, but the changed context and unforeseen surprises which lay ahead combined to create new ground. In the first place Britain was now a full European Community member, and in purely practical terms things were easier because English was now an official working language. Under the forthright Margaret Thatcher, however, the financial terms of Britain's entry agreement were under intense fire. She believed Britain had been fleeced in the entry arrangements and therefore that its assessed share of the EEC budget was unfair.

British media christened the Thatcher crusade as 'I want my money back'. There were, of course, contrary versions of the Thatcher story, but the very fervour of of the British campaign annoyed European governments. European Commission contacts in Brussels suggested privately to the New Zealand Mission, more than once, that Thatcher's zeal undermined British advocacy for New Zealand interests.

It had been only prudent for New Zealand to assume that once inside Europe, New Zealand's particular difficulties would not rate as the 'make or break' issue for the British that they had sometimes appeared to be during the entry negotiations themselves. British officials now occupying key jobs inside the European Commission (like Deputy Director-General of Agriculture) were not advocates for New Zealand. Moreover, those countries which had joined the European Community alongside Britain (farm producers like Ireland and Denmark) also had personnel now inside the tent. The head of the Commission's Dairy Directorate, for example, was 'an Irishman with a cause' (always a combustible combination), which was to cut New Zealand down to size, and there were Danes also spread through the the Commission's agricultural landscape. Denmark, as a dairy exporter itself, considered the special arrangements negotiated for New Zealand as part of Britain's entry package to have been at Danish expense.

Persistent New Zealand attempts ever since British enlargement to replicate the original 1972 five-year deal (which had expired in 1977) had, despite heroic efforts by Wellington officials and predecessors at the New Zealand Mission in Brussels, proven disappointing. A three-year extension to 1980, with further decreases in the quantities of butter, was secured. Trade offs between price and quantity (smaller tonnages for higher returns) formed part of ongoing dealings. But definitive arrangements for post 1980 proved more than EEC farm ministers, even with Britain as a member, could manage. Yearly rollovers were decided, and when even those became too hard to agree, the EEC resorted to monthly rollovers for permitted levels of New Zealand access. This made a mockery of predictability of trade for New Zealand producers.

At the same time New Zealand's problems as a global agricultural trader had magnified appreciably since British entry into Europe in 1973. Immense surplus of key commodities produced under the European Community's invidiously protective Common Agricultural Policy hung over world markets. By early 1984 there were a million tonnes of surplus European butter and 600,000 tonnes of beef in storage, as well as large stocks of other surplus products.

The price tag for producing, storing and disposing of such vast surpluses was monumental. There was snowballing demand inside the European Community, especially from finance ministries, for reform. That reinforced pressures, not surprisingly, to eliminate New Zealand levels of permitted trade access; and pressure as well to activate serious export competition to capture external dairy markets, at New Zealand expense, for the surplus European production.

New Zealand faced jeopardy on two fronts – it had to fight a rearguard action for diminishing access *into* Europe, and simultaneously fight against accelerating subsidised competition *from* Europe in world markets. The politics of all this consumed the efforts and energies of the Brussels Mission and shaped much of the diplomacy of New Zealand's network of European embassies, including Geneva.

Ministerial visits from Wellington were frequent, and often sudden. In April 1984, for example, the Mission received just two weeks' notice that Warren Cooper, as Foreign Minister, would visit all ten European capitals, and the Mission was instructed (not for the first time) to coordinate the overall programme with the other New Zealand missions in those capitals. That burden was additional to preparing the ground in respect to policy issues with the European Commission and others on its patch – the Belgian, Luxembourg and Danish authorities. Given the sheer intensity of the workload upon European politicians, the constant diplomatic task of oiling the wheels so as to open European doors, and then keep them open for visitors from Wellington (especially short-notice visitors), was not always fully understood or appreciated by visiting politicians, nor producer board chairmen and their senior advisers, who sometimes took ready access simply for granted.

Warren Cooper was a very different Foreign Minister from his predecessor, the urbane, experienced and senior Brian Talboys, whom he succeeded in 1981. He was a proud, self-made person who had been a house painter and sign writer, then mayor of Queenstown, before entering politics. As Foreign Minister he was not altogether comfortable with the worldly wise affectations of European politicians and (especially) officials. With his own officials he sometimes relished, apparently for the sake of it, taking the contrary view when presented with advice. His presentation of the New Zealand cause around the table with the Europeans was unvarnished, although cables back to Wellington reporting on his various encounters jazzed things up a bit.

The Brussels visit on this particular occasion had its moments. Warren Cooper was a keen jogger, and New Zealand overseas missions had been alerted always to ensure allowance for this activity in the ministerial visit programme. Upon arrival with accompanying officials at the Sheraton Hotel in downtown Brussels, Cooper announced immediately that he intended to go for a jog. The Belgians had assigned a security detail to the New Zealand Minister, and the Mission had suggested that they include suitably athletic minders to keep up with Mr Cooper, who duly appeared clad in a T-shirt emblazoned with a 'Visit Queenstown' motif and a pair of brief but striking semi-gloss shorts with the New Zealand flag front and back. On the face of it, such togs seemed to affirm a New Zealand Foreign Minister who was willing to go that extra mile for his country. I introduced him to the Belgian security detail, who had suggested to me beforehand that they would take a right out of the the hotel and head toward Brussels' attractive old city square. When I indicated this to the Minister, he, true to form, responded that he wanted instead to take a left out of the hotel. There was a flicker of dismay on the face of the head of the security detail as Cooper brushed past him.

The Sheraton Hotel stood at the very boundary of the Brussels red-light district, and taking a left out the front door led straight to rows of buildings whose large illuminated front windows displayed women with inviting enticements and suggestive gestures. The mind's-eye picture of the New Zealand Foreign Minister loping through the streets amidst such allurement, with the national flag decorating his loins, provided some light relief from the doleful duty of safeguarding New Zealand trade interests in the 'capital of Europe'. After the jog Cooper himself remarked upon the somewhat bizarre exposure.

In the background to that visit there was increasing criticism inside the European Commission about the institutionalised but informal dairy cooperation with New Zealand, the product of the original British entry agreement (the so-called Luxembourg Protocol), whereby the enlarged European Community undertook not to frustrate New Zealand efforts to diversify markets away from Europe. Such cooperation in Brussels buttressed the International Dairy Arrangement in Geneva. The New Zealand Dairy Board was present around the table in both places. This was the product of gentle New Zealand diplomatic persuasion, and was intended to supply 'belt and braces' protection for New Zealand's dairy export economy. In both places, however, mutual trust between European Commission officials and the New Zealand Dairy Board was receding.

That pot was being stirred by the European Commission's Director-General for Agriculture in Brussels, an appropriately named Frenchman, Claude Villain. He came direct from central casting in the role of wily French manipulator, with rimless spectacles and mirthless gaze, who sought throughout to privilege French interests absolutely. Villain exercised considerable influence over his nominal boss, the quiet, unassuming and somewhat indecisive Danish Commissioner for Agriculture, Poul Dalsager.

Terence in 1938 with his parents, Paddy and Peggy, and his sister Bridget.

Terence joins the New Zealand Department of External Affairs in 1959, aged 23.

As Second Secretary, New Zealand Embassy to Thailand, at the Special Conference on Asian Economic Cooperation (ECAFE), Manila, 2–5 December 1963, with Foss Shanahan (left) and Geoff Easterbrook-Smith (right).

'When Joe met Joe.' Reestablishment of diplomatic relations with China: Chinese Premier Zhou Enlai and New Zealand Foreign Minister Joe Walding (centre front) with their delegations on a visit to China in 1973. Terence is second from right in front row; Bryce Harland, New Zealand Ambassador to China, third from left; Geoff Easterbrook-Smith fourth from right.

Terence and Elizabeth at the opening of the Chinese Embassy in Wellington with Pei Jianzhang, the first Chinese Ambassador to New Zealand, in 1975.

As New Zealand High Commissioner to the Cook Islands, welcoming New Zealand Foreign Minister Rt Hon Brian Talboys (centre) to Rarotonga, with Cook Islands Internal Affairs Minister Tupui Henry (left), January 1977.

Meeting with Cook Islands Cabinet, 30 May 1977. Cook Islands Prime Minister
Sir Albert Henry is at the head of the table, flanked by Terence O'Brien (right) and
New Zealand Prime Minister Robert Muldoon (left).

Escorting New Zealand Prime Minister Robert Muldoon (centre) and his entourage
on a fishing trip, Rarotonga, May 1977.

Presentation of credentials to Gaston Thorn, President of the European Commission, April 1983.

As New Zealand Ambassador to the European Economic Community in Brussels, 1984, with New Zealand Trade Minister Mike Moore (right) and Deputy Secretary of the Department of Trade and Industry, Geoff Easterbrook-Smith (left).

At the Apple and Pear Board cool store opening, Brussels, 26 February 1985.

Terence and Elizabeth
meet Belgian King
Baudouin and Queen
Fabiola, January 1985.

With New Zealand Minister of Foreign Affairs Russell Marshall on a Pacific Islands visit in the late 1980s.

With the President of Palau, Lazarus Salii, in his office in Koror, Palau, 4 July 1988.

With New Zealand Prime Minister David Lange (right) and Niue Premier Robert Rex (left) at the New Zealand Residence in Apia, Samoa, for the 1987 South Pacific Forum.

At a Korean National Day party at GATT headquarters in Geneva, with the Deputy Secretary of the Department of Trade and Industry, Ted Woodfield, in the early 1980s.

With Deputy Foreign Minister Fran Wilde (centre) on a visit to Bourail, New Caledonia, 12 October 1987.

Prime Ministers David Lange and Bob Hawke with their wives Naomi and Hazel at the Sydney Bicentennial presentation of the cutter *Akarana*, a gift from New Zealand to Australia, 20 August 1988. The *Akarana* is in the background.

With Deputy Prime Minister Geoffrey Palmer on a plane to New Caledonia for the funeral of assassinated Kanak leader Jean-Marie Tjibaou in May 1989.

At the United Nations with UN Secretary-General Javier Pérez de Cuéllar, 1991.

After New Zealand's UN Security Council election win, in Western European & Others Group, beating Spain, then Sweden, 1992.

Terence after winning a seat on the UN Security Council – when asked how he reacted to the win, Jim Bolger told the press: 'He's up in the air about it.' (Tom Scott cartoon, *Evening Post*, 1992).

Banging the gavel as United Nations Security Council President, March 1993, with UN Secretary-General Boutros Boutros-Ghali beside him, and behind them Permanent New Zealand Representative to the United Nations Gerard van Bohemen (left) and Deputy Ambassador John McKinnon (centre).

At the United Nations with 'Honest Jim' Bolger, New Zealand Prime Minister, and Hilary Willberg, Deputy Permanent Representative to the United Nations, early 1990s.

With United States President George H. W. Bush and New Zealand Prime Minister Jim Bolger at the Waldorf Astoria Hotel, New York, 23 September 1991.

Trying to get some sleep on a United Nations plane to Bosnia as a member of the UN Security Council, April 1993.

With Chinese Foreign Minister Qian Qichen at the New Zealand Residence in New York, October 1992.

With Prime Minister Jim Bolger and New Zealand diplomats Jane Coombs and Peter Kennedy outside the United Nations building on 46th Street, New York, early 1990s.

With South Korean Minister of Foreign Affairs Han Sung-joo, mid-1990s.

Terence with his children (John top left; Daniel, Georgia and Timothy left to right) at the New Zealand Residence in Geneva, early 1980s.

The O'Brien family in 2011 (left to right): John (42), Dan (36), Terence (74), Georgia (39), Tim (34), and Elizabeth (71).

Terence and Elizabeth on their wedding day, with Ambassador Sir Stephen Weir, at his residence in Thailand, 5 August 1963.

Terence and Elizabeth in front of their newly built retirement home, Raumati Beach, March 2014.

As Director of the New Zealand Centre for Strategic Studies, on a visit to North Korea, 1998.

At an NZIIA/Diplosphere conference with Maty Nikkhou-O'Brien (NZIIA), Robert Ayson (CSS), and Jonathan Sinclair (British Ambassador), 2015.

Terence with Andrew Wilford, recipient of the Terence O'Brien Scholarship, 2022.

Villain's dealings with the New Zealand Mission were always correct. Visiting Wellington-based trade officials, or at least some of them, sometimes took a charitable view of him in the hope of more accommodating treatment for New Zealand. Those hopes were out of tune with reality. Indeed, Villain compounded the felony by championing a proposal for an EEC sheep meat regulation to be linked to any new New Zealand butter deal. The two issues had previously, by mutual acknowledgement, been kept entirely separate.

The vexatious procrastination of European farm ministers about a definitive decision on future New Zealand butter access, described above, meant a decision was put off to mid-1984. On 1 January 1984, France assumed Chair of the European Farm Council. With Villain in the wings manufacturing ammunition, New Zealand was destined for rough going. An entirely unforeseen factor then intruded with the decision by Prime Minister Robert Muldoon to call a snap election for 14 July 1984. That immediately raised the complication of a clash with the timing of the scheduled mid-year decision from European farm ministers about access arrangements for New Zealand butter. The omens were not promising.

When I arrived in Brussels in the first half of 1983, the prime task was to persuade the European Commission to table a definitive proposal for predictable five-year New Zealand butter access. Failing that, the prospect for short-term rollover arrangements from the beginning of 1984 was a distinct possibility. Considerable New Zealand persuasion was exerted on the Agricultural Commissioner in Brussels, and in New Zealand when he had himself visited, to resurrect a five-year proposal. He had an undisclosed proposition in his hip pocket but was loath to produce it. Ireland flatly opposed the notion of a multi-year arrangement. Others like the Danes were equivocal; and the French were determined to link any arrangement to a curb of New Zealand's sheep meat trade. Inside the European Community the British were not able to loosen the logjam.

Given the undeniably political character of the New Zealand access problem, New Zealand suggested a definitive decision should be referred to European foreign ministers, not farm ministers. That was resisted, including by the British. Whitehall's number one political objective remained a reduction in the UK budgetary contribution. Placing New

Zealand access issues on the foreign ministers' agenda would, in British minds, be a distraction. All of this resulted in no definitive agreement by the EEC about New Zealand access as from 1 January 1984; we faced yet more short-term rollovers. This prompted some angry letters from Muldoon and Cooper to their European counterparts.

The European farm ministers meeting scheduled for 18 June 1984 in Luxembourg, just four weeks before the New Zealand election, was to be the occasion for a definitive EEC decision on future New Zealand access. Every New Zealand sinew had to be bent over the lead-up period to persuade Commissioner Dalsager and his minions to produce the right proposal. The outcome could well become a factor in the New Zealand election outcome. In the normal course, a New Zealand minister would have likely been despatched to be in the wings while European ministers deliberated, in order to defend the New Zealand corner. But with a general election imminent that would not now be happening. The instruction to me from Wellington was therefore 'to engage and pursue' in the corridors at Luxembourg. Before the meeting the fervour and intensity of the New Zealand Mission dealings in Brussels sharpened considerably.

Despite prior agreement with key European Commission officials, the British Minister and his delegation to maintain close contact throughout, communication proved erratic and complex. There was moreover no line of secure communication with Wellington. A whole spate of telephone calls from the lobby of the Holiday Inn across the road from the Kirchberg Conference Centre, on an open line, was the sum total of our connexion, as negotiations ebbed and flowed day and night (I spent over 10,000 Belgian francs on the calls). Brian Smythe from the New Zealand Mission, who had good contacts amongst the delegations, patrolled the corridors at the Kirchberg, keeping track on overall progress.

An account of the European haggling required to produce an outcome for New Zealand is hardly relevant now. A five-year framework was finally agreed but with actual quantities of butter only set for the first three, requiring a further Commission proposal when the time came. The Irish had remained adamantly opposed to a full five-year commitment on quantities. I was instructed over the open telephone line in the late hours to signify New Zealand assent to an understanding with the Europeans about sheep meat, allowing governments (i.e. France) to claim 'sensitive market' status, and thereby regulate New Zealand imports.

The outcome was a curate's egg but New Zealand could feel generally satisfied and on the eve of New Zealand's election, it was portrayed by Wellington as a success for the government. From a personal standpoint, the result meant yet more trench warfare in prospect to cover butter quantities left blank for years four and five of the Kirchberg deal. But in terms of immediate effect, the result at Luxembourg had no positive bearing whatsoever on the New Zealand election. The Muldoon Government lost.

CR

The election of the David Lange Government brought into office a younger generation of politicians whose world view did not embrace Europe in the same way as their predecessors. Some premonition of this had occurred in Brussels, when Lange had visited and stayed under our roof in early 1984 as Leader of the Opposition. Both in conversation and in a lively discussion with the European Commission President Gaston Thorn, Lange had lamented how the New Zealand–European relationship was so monopolised by issues of dairy and meat trade that it consumed New Zealand's political and diplomatic energies to the exclusion of other opportunities and interests that better reflected New Zealand's evolving sense of place in the world.

That message was conveyed after the election to all of New Zealand's European ambassadors, who were were summoned to London in September 1984 to meet with the new Prime Minister. Officials accompanying David Lange advised ambassadors separately of Wellington's intention to slim down New Zealand's representation in Europe. Behind that advice, it seemed, was a conclusion that Europe was in a state of secular decline. It was true that much was being written at the time, by pundits in Paris, Bonn, Rome and elsewhere, about 'Europessimism' or 'Eurosclerosis'.

A straw in the wind was the 1985 MFA Annual Report (the first under the new government), which made no mention of Europe. Yet any notion that New Zealand could write off the European Community was mistaken. It was important to realise that the Lange Government had been spared as it took office by the cliffhanging result at Luxembourg about New Zealand access to the European market, because it avoided an immediate jump into abrasive trench warfare with the Europeans. That was a reprieve for the new Trade Minister Mike Moore, although he did not necessarily recognise it as such.

Key policies announced by the Lange Government attracted note in several European quarters. The neo-liberal free market agenda of Rogernomics sparked interest, witnessed by the early first visit to Brussels by Mike Moore. A lunch arranged to meet him attracted EEC Commission top brass. He treated the assembled notables to what one distinguished New Zealand journalist has since described as his professional hallmark: 'an engaging but often mystifying stream-of-consciousness ode to free trade.'

But it was the new government's non-nuclear policy that drew most notice. There was at the time notable controversy throughout much of Europe over the intended installation of a new American cruise missile system, as part of the United States' anti-Soviet deterrence policy. Large anti-nuclear marches were occurring in many cities, Brussels included. It was not exactly surprising then that the non-nuclear decisions of distant New Zealand, and the hostile American reaction, attracted notice amongst European governments, concerned lest New Zealand's example 'infect' the attitudes in their streets.

Located as it was in the 'capital of Europe', with the headquarters of both the European Commission and the North Atlantic Treaty Organisation (NATO) on its patch, the Brussels Mission was readily conscious of the coincidence between New Zealand trading interests and its non-nuclear policy. As American disapproval of New Zealand's nuclear 'disease', with its potential to complicate decisions about European cruise missile installation, heightened the temperature, it became clear that New Zealand was 'being talked about' in NATO. The New Zealand Mission learnt that visits to Brussels by the Australian Prime Minister Bob Hawke and Foreign Minister Bill Hayden had included discussions about 'unreliable allies' and effects upon stability in the Pacific.

I began to acquire invitations for diplomatic hospitality from the NATO end of town. Given the Mission's usual fixation on agricultural trade problems with the European Community at the other end of town, this additional socialising was a novel experience for me. My encounters with North Atlantic Treaty ambassadors and officials included a meeting with the NATO Secretary-General, Lord Carrington. Early on he suggested a 'drop by for a chat'. In his charming, intelligent and mildly patrician way, he courteously enquired what actually was going on in New Zealand, and the reasons for New Zealand policy, and when would it all end?

Until this point the New Zealand Mission had received little considered guidance from Wellington (other than texts of ministerial statements and speeches) about how embassies and high commissions were to carry, defend and explain the new policy. Official guidance, such as it was, instructed the Mission to take a low key approach with NATO contacts, and to emphasise that New Zealand remained an active, self-reliant, committed member of the 'western community'. Yet queries from those contacts persisted: 'Just how long will this New Zealand policy last? When will New Zealand return to the western security fold?'

It was not hard to explain the policy in broad terms as a democratic choice by a country with a record of democracy every bit as distinguished and venerable as any in Europe or North America. It was, however, slightly harder to explain (in the absence of considered guidance) why New Zealand was opting to enshrine the policy in its law. The objective set out in my original letter of appointment was, after all, 'to strengthen politico-economic relations with the EEC' (that letter had, of course, been signed out by the previous New Zealand government). Inside the Mission we were aware of high-level dealings in Washington, and with leaders in London, Bonn and the Hague, by Deputy Prime Minister Geoffrey Palmer. But detailed information was tightly held at the New Zealand end, for understandable reasons. NATO delegations, on the other hand, were kept in the loop by the Americans.

Our contacts persistently cautioned New Zealand against heedlessly unravelling 'the seamless web of western security'. That argument perhaps flattered the extent of New Zealand's influence, but it was for the most part advice diligently given. Repetition grew wearisome, however, particularly as we battled with unceasing, abrasive European intransigence over farm trade at the other end of town in European Commission headquarters.

I cleared my own mind in an exchange with the Commission's Director-General of External Relations, formerly a senior member of the UK Foreign Office and an important Brussels contact with whom we regularly shared hospitality. One evening, when liquid refreshment had been partaken, the Director-General launched point blank into the 'seamless web of western security' argument, employing colourful and unflattering language to describe New Zealand, its prime minister and its deluded non-nuclear policy.

I was sufficiently moved to reply that the 'seamless web of western security' could not surely be a one-way street; it applied not just to political security but also to economic security – especially for a small, democratic, dependable, trade-reliant nation like New Zealand. Yet the EEC treated New Zealand abysmally when it came to European market access (even down to measly monthly rollovers for permitted butter exports), while it strove to capture markets from New Zealand with its own heavily subsidised farm exports – something it had explicitly promised not to do under the terms of the British entry treaty. That behaviour, mirrored equally by US protectionism, was obviously heedless of New Zealand security. It would be entirely wrong to suggest the Director-General's opinions were in influenced by any of this. He was treating me to a brisk dose of European realpolitik. We parted cordially. Our regular official contacts remained intact.

The Lange Government had introduced a somewhat puzzling re-arrangement of ministerial responsibilities for New Zealand external relations. The Prime Minister retained the foreign affairs portfolio for himself. Direct ministerial responsibility for European dealings, however, was split amongst a triumvirate – Mike Moore as Trade Minister assumed overall big-picture responsibility, Frank O'Flynn as Deputy Foreign Minister and Minister of Defence was allocated day-to-day oversight, and Colin Moyle as Agriculture Minister was bestowed with concern for actual dairy, meat and fruit access questions. It was a crowded turf.

Mike Moore's preference was for leadership of large trade/business delegations and a celebrity role of 'opening doors' politically for New Zealand commercial interests. The creation of a new Overseas Marketing Board was his priority. Trench combat in Brussels was not really his scene. As far as Frank O'Flynn was concerned, bestowing day-to-day responsibility for EEC relations on someone with the rank of Deputy Foreign Affairs Minister, whatever that actually meant in practice, did not resonate readily in European capitals, particularly when New

Zealand diplomatic missions were tasked to arrange visits by O'Flynn. Based upon actual ministerial performance in Brussels by each of the trio, Colin Moyle displayed the readiest grasp of the complexities involved for New Zealand.

On the nuclear policy the Lange Government took early steps to test the waters in Denmark, which had established a policy of excluding nuclear-armed vessels from its ports while remaining a loyal NATO member. Were there lessons here for New Zealand? As New Zealand's non-resident Ambassador to Denmark, I accompanied Defence Minister and Deputy Foreign Minister Frank O'Flynn when he visited Copenhagen with foreign affairs advisers from Wellington, ten weeks after the New Zealand election. O'Flynn was an older Cabinet member amongst the generation of 'young Turks' now in charge in Wellington. He was temperamentally different and, it was said, did not enjoy the entire confidence of the Prime Minister.

It was true Denmark had a ban on nuclear-armed vessels in its ports, but (unlike the proposed New Zealand law) it did not require prior confirmation from visiting vessels that they were not carrying nuclear weapons. The Danes assumed that friends and allies, fully aware of Danish policy, would act accordingly. Their Foreign Minister Uffe Ellemann-Jensen, a former TV celebrity with a cardboard smile, went out of his way in his meeting with O'Flynn to differentiate the respective positions of the two countries. He subsequently visited New Zealand in late 1985, where he repeated this 'same but different' message.

Interest in the O'Flynn visit and New Zealand's non-nuclear policy amongst a widely supportive Danish public and parliament was reflected in his well attended press conference. Besides Danish media, in the front row were representatives of the principal Soviet news organs, TASS and Izvestia. The Mission forewarned the Minister, but in response to one query about American attitudes to the New Zealand policy, Flynn unburdened himself, berating US reactions intemperately. The Soviet media scribbled furiously. All told, it was not a particularly famous diplomatic performance. I visited Copenhagen frequently and the nuclear issue invariably figured in many encounters. The last occasion was with Prime Minister David Lange in May 1986, by which time other confounding factors, as explained below, had intruded into the calculations.

Reaction to the New Zealand nuclear policy surfaced at the European Parliament in Strasbourg. The Parliament's influence over European affairs, at least at that time, should not be exaggerated. But it was prudent that New Zealand not ignore regular calls from Strasbourg for New Zealand agricultural exports to be eliminated from the the European market. A two-member (one government and one opposition) New Zealand parliamentary delegation visited Strasbourg in February 1985. In keeping with custom, the New Zealand Mission extended support to the visiting New Zealand parliamentarians.

The small New Zealand delegation (Paul East MP and Margaret Shields MP) quickly encountered expressions of disapproval about the New Zealand non-nuclear policy, and claims by European critics that this provided yet another reason to eliminate access for New Zealand farm exports. The government member of the delegation sturdily defended the nuclear policy. The opposition member consorted with European Parliamentary members to draft a resolution flatly opposing New Zealand's policy. Lending appropriate support to this particular delegation provided a real agility test for the New Zealand Mission.

And then came the *Rainbow Warrior*. Amongst unforeseeable factors affecting New Zealand–Europe relations, this took the biscuit. In July 1985 the Greenpeace vessel *Rainbow Warrior* was blown up in Auckland Harbour. Suspicion over French involvement was rife. But it was not until early August that an official statement from Paris confirmed their secret service (DGSE) had been implicated, and that a full and swift investigation was under way. New Zealand police had captured two of the DGSE agents. The result of the French investigation (the so-called Tricot Report) was released in barely three weeks. It amounted to a whitewash, and was widely condemned as such even in France, and of course by PM David Lange.

In Brussels we occupied a dress-circle seat watching the convulsions south of the Belgian border. We consumed the French newspapers daily, some whom asserted the New Zealand Prime Minister was seizing upon the incident in order to 'chase France from the Pacific'. Another asserted that New Zealand had clandestine sources in Paris – 'a mole in the Élysee' was the claim. Early on, under advice from Wellington, the Mission sought diplomatic protection from Belgian security services; there was concern lest right-wing French elements seek to kidnap New

Zealand diplomats from somewhere in Europe (not just France) as a bargaining chip in return for release of the DGSE agents, due for trial in November.

Brussels was a potential target as our Mission was housed in the Banque National de Paris building. Inside the Mission some welcomed the Belgian security assistance. Our longstanding Embassy driver, Achille Gravensteyn, someone with strong Formula One instincts (and with whom several visiting New Zealand ministers and officials had experienced white-knuckle rides in the course of business), revelled in the emergency evasive speed driving instruction provided by Belgian security. He then incorporated this knowledge into his regular behind-the-wheel driving repetoire. A similar, rather more sinister incident involved the removal overnight, by oxy-acetylene torch, of the petrol tank from a parked New Zealand official car, a BMW. According to Belgian and other security investigators this bore the signature of the Irish Republican Army, with its record of cutting out petrol tanks, loading them with explosives, and then installing them in similar models belonging to targeted individuals.

The *Rainbow Warrior* incident inevitably linked the fate of the French prisoners in Auckland to New Zealand trade access both to France and to Europe more widely. Coincidental decisions about extension of the New Zealand butter access arrangement for 1986/87, where France's vote would be critical, were looming larger. In the wake of *Rainbow Warrior* the French provocatively imposed extra restraints upon New Zealand lamb sales into their own market, and New Zealand, for the first time, lodged objections before GATT in Geneva, thereby involving the European Commission awkwardly in the gathering New Zealand–France dispute.

From Brussels and other European capitals, New Zealand diplomatic reporting warned Wellington that contacts were urging New Zealand not to pursue redress with France in ways that might involve her European partners being obliged to take sides – because New Zealand would be the loser. It is instructive to recall, a generation and a half later, when terrorism is widely and consistently condemned, that not one 'western' protest was lodged over the French misdeeds in Auckland at that time; yet they amounted to an act of state-backed terror. New Zealand diplomatic missions could, and did, respond to European officials' admonitions in terms that New Zealand trusted equally there would be no support inside Europe for French vindictiveness towards New Zealand.

The first steps by New Zealand and France to resolve these differences were discreet. In Brussels the Mission was not in the loop, although a visit by the Deputy MFA Secretary Chris Beeby to European capitals in September 1985 shed some light. At the same time a meeting between Deputy PM Geoffrey Palmer and French Foreign Minister Roland Dumas (the first high-level exchange since *Rainbow Warrior*) in New York on the margins of the UN General Assembly provided signals of movement. Geoffrey Palmer had just completed an unfruitful round of talks in Washington with the Americans on NZ–US relations, which he recounts in his 2018 biography *Reform*, published by Victoria University Press.

It was hard to escape the fact that in some European eyes the New Zealand image at this time was blemished – relations with France were soured, while affinity with the US was unfastened. European contacts in several capitals were urging New Zealand diplomatic representatives to mend fences in both directions, sometimes in the course of the same conversation. Meanwhile the complexity about future New Zealand dairy trade access into the European Community loomed ever closer.

All things considered, a prime ministerial visit to Europe by David Lange in mid-1986 was fitting and expedient. The New Zealand Mission was tasked with coordinating arrangements with other New Zealand embassies for the visit, which took in five countries and the EEC Commission, but not France. It was a complex task. Formal discussions in Brussels included a three-hour round table with the full slate of EEC Commissioners led by its new French president, Jacques Delors, that covered an impressive range of current foreign and domestic themes, although the issue of France–New Zealand relations did not feature directly. A side-purpose of the PM's visit was to brief me about progress on reconciling differences with France, and how that process was to be dovetailed with the prospective European Community decision on the terms of the 1986/87 New Zealand butter exports to the Community.

My one-on-one briefing with the PM (which occurred at the Hotel Amigo in central Brussels) was full of wit and humour. Mr Lange was a formidable raconteur, but not a natural born briefer. For someone conditioned by the prosaic ways of diplomacy it was a little difficult at times to grasp the quick-witted gist. The PM also presumed knowledge that the New Zealand Mission did not have. He explained the choreography proposed for France–New Zealand reconciliation: mediation by the UN Secretary-General Pérez de Cuéllar, plus monetary compensation by France, and French acceptance of 1986/87 butter access for New Zealand in terms of the 1984 European Commission proposal; all that in return for repatriation of the imprisoned French agents.

It was obvious New Zealand had no interest in prolonged differences with France. Under the terms of the proposed *Rainbow Warrior* settlement, however, the French were actually agreeing to do nothing new in relation to butter access – they had agreed in 1984 to the five-year formula, and to the full quantities then proposed by the European Commission, including for 1987/88. It was the Irish who had blocked the deal.

As explained by the PM, there would be no inference or language in the envisaged text of the *Rainbow Warrior* settlement that affirmed the continuing interest that New Zealand retained in the European market; and that this stretched out beyond a simple 1987 timeframe. From a Brussels and New Zealand trade policy perspective at least, it was reasonable (and logical) that France be asked to recognise that fact. The omission was registered with the PM at the Hotel Amigo. But the die was cast. Lawyers in Wellington had presumably concluded that such a provision was more than the traffic could bear.

It had been decided that David Lange would only give one press conference throughout his whirlwind 1986 European expedition, and that this would be in Brussels. It was a masterful performance in front a large group of what was surely one of the best press corps anywhere and was right up there with Lange's famous Oxford Union debate as he parried questions on nuclear policy, French relations, US attitudes to New Zealand, his perceptions of Europe, and so on. The London *Financial Times* correspondent, a battle-hardened veteran and valued source for the New Zealand Mission, remarked privately afterwards that of the literally hundreds of media briefings with the great and the good, which he had attended over the years in the EEC press room, he had not experienced anything to compare.

There were flashes of Lange's irreverent humour elsewhere. In Copenhagen, which he visited after Brussels, and following his meetings with political leaders (where once again notes were compared on non-nuclear policy, and on ANZUS, *Rainbow Warrior*, etc.), he was guest of the Danish Foreign Minister at a dinner in the famous Tivoli Gardens, where he spent a good half hour prior on the amusements sporting a funny hat, while his press secretary raced about beseeching media not to photograph the escapade. The dining room was itself a model of Danish style and contemporary design, including some beautiful modern chandeliers by the famed Danish silversmith Georg Jensen. As the guests took their seats, the chandeliers slowly lowered until they hung just over the gleaming white tablecloths and stylish place settings. The PM gazed, as everyone did, in admiration at this spectacle and then murmured audibly to his host alongside: 'Are the CIA joining us for dinner, then?' The ebullient Danish Foreign Minister was, for once, lost for words.

In the immediate aftermath of the Lange visit, the New Zealand Mission strove to ensure at senior levels that things in Brussels moved in the way envisaged by the France–New Zealand agreement brokered under the UN Secretary-General. The Commissioner for Agriculture, Frans Andriessen, warned more than once that the farm ministers would assuredly protest against outside interference (by the UN Secretary-General or anyone else) in domestic decision making about European and farm policy. So it proved, and some of it was acrimonious. After some cliff-hanging, Andriessen finally produced the 'right' proposal for 1986/87 butter access, which was endorsed with minor adjustment by European farm ministers.

As backup we had also secured agreement that foreign ministers under British chairmanship would have the final say. This had required close interaction with the British Permanent Representative to the EEC, David Hannay, who had proved initially resistant to the idea. He was a demanding personality not troubled by self doubt. Interestingly, our paths would cross again subsequently in New York, including on the UN Security Council. The last-minute anxieties and uncertainty provided a curtain call as I was winding up my assignment to Brussels, to be replaced by my able successor, Gerry Thompson. I was asked to delay departure until the settlement was on the point of being achieved, so once again Elizabeth and our four children set off without me, but we caught up in Africa as we passed through.

ଔ

The Brussels job was not confined exclusively to head banging over butter, lamb or cheese. The accomplishments of the New Zealand Apple and Pear Marketing Board were exemplary. They handled relations with the EEC Commission in a masterful way, and the opening of a large cool store on the wharves at the Belgian port of Zeebrugge, which served as the Board's distribution point for all reefer ship cargoes to continental Europe, was a testament to their accomplishments; in particular to the trust that they succeeded in building with the EEC Commission.

The responsibilities of the Embassy to Belgium extended beyond preoccupations with the EEC grocery basket, and included ANZAC Day commemorations, held yearly in Flanders at Messines and Ypres, as well as the cemeteries at Passchendaele and Ploegsteert. World War II commemorations, on the other hand, were not as significant, since New Zealand's principal military contribution in Europe occurred in Italy. I was fortunate to participate, however, in one moving World War II commemoration at the small Flemish town of Overpelt, near the Belgian–German border.

The purpose was to unveil a small stained-glass window in the local church which commemorates the heroic actions of a Kiwi pilot from the RAF 75 Squadron whose Lancaster bomber was shot down by a German night fighter on return from a raid over Dortmund in 1944. The badly damaged Lancaster was in grave danger of crashing into the small town when the pilot, Flying Officer Burke from Taranaki, ordered his crew to bail out, then turned the aircraft towards nearby marshland and crashed, killing himself in the process.

A small group of townspeople in Overpelt discovered the remnants of the Lancaster quite a long while later, and dedicated their efforts to creating a suitable commemoration for this act of bravery. In the small town church they installed a stained-glass window depicting a Māori warrior, with the squadron crest 'Ake Ake, Kia Kaha'. There can be few such Māori windows elsewhere on continental Europe. The unveiling ceremony included the pilot's sister from Taranaki, flown to Belgium courtesy of the RNZAF, as well as New Zealand's senior military attaché from London. There was a good turnout of British 75 Squadron veterans, and a convivial post-ceremony celebration.

My final ANZAC Day ceremony at Messines/Ypres was in 1986. After morning visits to their respective cemeteries, the New Zealand and Australian contingents traditionally met up with the town councillors at the famous Menin gate in Ypres for a 'Last Post' ceremony, and then repaired to city hall for a mayoral reception. After that the New Zealand and Australian ambassadors hosted a lunch, taking turn about each year, at a restaurant chosen by the Ypres Mayor, who customarily chose only the best.

That year it was the reputable Cheval Noir in central Ypres. New Zealand was in the chair. The lunch proved once again to be a lengthy convivial marathon. As dusk approached, and proceedings were still in full swing, the Cheval Noir chef entered ceremoniously to loud applause from the civic fathers, wearing a tall white hat and bearing a very large cake with sizeable New Zealand and Australian flags on top, fashioned in icing sugar. This was clamorously greeted by the assembled fathers, who commanded with one voice that the trans-Tasman envoys stand and consume their flags, which were respectively handed to us both. We rose to enthusiastic applause and chomped away. It was a final curtain.

The family had passed three years in the bucolic, thatched-roof New Zealand residence in the inner suburb of Woluwe-Saint-Pierre, situated alongside an attractive park where tobogganing in the snow was a winter pastime. Given the house's location it was fairly easy to lure EEC Commission heavyweights and others to lunches and dinners, and it was comfortable as a family home. There was, however, one narrow squeak with the thatched roof.

I was seated in my office at the end of a working day when I received a frantic telephone call from Elizabeth, asking me to come quickly. I arrived speedily to see four fire engines and squads of firemen around the garden, and hoses everywhere. A children's birthday party involving fireworks had gone wrong. One parachute flare had landed on the thatch on the reverse side of the roof, and was at first not noticed. A burly Flemish fire chief confronted me with the words 'You are very lucky indeed, in a matter of minutes the fire would have been out of control'. The children were mortified and shaken. Mario the Portugese housekeeper had courageously climbed a ladder to the fire, and attempted to beat it out. This helped save us from the worst. The thought that we might have had to inform Wellington headquarters that we had burnt down their only thatched piece of real estate haunted our imagination!

8. HOMELAND

I had petitioned the Secretary of Foreign Affairs, Merv Norrish, for responsibilities post-Brussels that were quite removed from trade policy. He assented. I was assigned as Assistant Secretary supervising relations with Australia, the South Pacific, and (for a short while) the United States, as well as the New Zealand ODA programme. It added up to a stimulating experience that lasted four years. That was good too because the family had only lived two years in New Zealand out of the previous ten. We had missed the divisive Springbok rugby tour, the death throes of the Muldoon Government, the first impacts throughout New Zealand of Rogernomics, the break with the US over nuclear policy, the visit of US Secretary of State George Shultz where he redefined New Zealand as a 'friend but not an ally' of the US, plus the controversy surrounding the non-visit of the frigate USS *Buchanan* – and much else.

Those events imbued work at the Ministry of External Relations and Trade (MERT) with a certain tension, particularly work involving New Zealand relationships with Australia and the South Pacific. The Australians remained strongly averse to New Zealand's non-nuclear policy, bewailing the consequences it had for the Australia–New Zealand–United States (ANZUS) security treaty, which the Americans had decided was no longer operable with New Zealand, as far as they were concerned.

In addition and coincidentally, defence policy reviews were scheduled in both countries at this time and provided potential for sharpened trans-Tasman sensitivities. In the same vein, the first comprehensive five-year review of the 1983 Closer Economic Relationship (CER) was due in 1988. The political, security and trade agendas of the trans-Tasman relationship were therefore loaded. The political chemistry was awkward, and the respective prime ministers (Hawke and Lange) held each other in low esteem, although that was not a first in the history of trans-Tasman connexions.

In the South Pacific, anxiety was expressed about disagreements between New Zealand and the US over nuclear policy. Some governments, like the Cook Islands, openly criticised New Zealand policy, but most did not sheet home blame; rather they expressed concern over the fall out between two friends of the South Pacific. Given that New Zealand's understanding of, and accomplishments in, the region were judged in Wellington to embellish the country's international credentials, there was an unmistakable need to 'up the New Zealand game'. Above all, non-nuclear New Zealand needed to demonstrate a capacity to 'take pains' in the South Pacific in ways that larger powers (and this included Australia) were unable to because of wider and grander objectives.

The levels of New Zealand aid in the region and the number of New Zealand diplomatic staff assigned to the South Pacific had actually been declining. Moreover, other New Zealand government departments with historically supportive connexions inside the South Pacific were now divesting themselves of those responsibilities, because the public sector reforms of the Lange Government demanded that departments concentrate domestically on core business. Radio New Zealand shortwave broadcasting into the South Pacific, for example, was being curtailed as a cost-cutting measure; and other activities like aerial navigational calibration in the region, prized by South Pacific governments for the physical connexions they provided to distant outer islands, was being privatised. MERT found itself frequently sidelined from such decision making, which was being driven out of the Treasury.

There was the real need for a policy rebuild. Revision of the aid programme was an obvious priority. Regularised official-level consultations on political, security and economic issues were initiated (Australia had no equivalent); an Associate New Zealand Minister of Foreign Affairs with special Pacific Islands responsibility (Fran Wilde) was appointed; New Zealand's first Māori Governor-General (Sir Paul Reeves) paid a wide-ranging visit into the region (whose scope exceeded all such previous expeditions); and a nine-person South Pacific policy review ('Towards a Pacific Islands Community') was commissioned by Geoffrey Palmer, who succeeded David Lange as Prime Minister in

August 1989. This review took six months, and visited (with the help of the RNZAF) every Pacific Islands Forum member country, as well as the French territories.

The Reeves expedition fell short of the Ministry's fondest hopes when the publicity about it was entirely swamped by the news of Sir Paul's ritual pig killing in the home village of the Vanuatu Prime Minister, Walter Lini – a special honour, but one seized upon by New Zealand animal rights groups as totally unacceptable behaviour. His ministerial advisers, who included me as the accompanying Assistant Secretary, had advised him to perform the ritual. The Royal Society for the Prevention of Cruelty to Animals in New Zealand demanded that Sir Paul immediately surrender his patronage of their organisation. There were other sensitivities too, of which Sir Paul was clearly aware, deriving from the very fact he was the first Māori Governor-General on such a wide-ranging expedition to the region. In Tonga, for example, his initial reception bordered on discourteous.

New Zealand's diplomatic reach was extended in the region by establishing formal ties with Micronesia, the Marshall Islands and Palau, who had all in the early 1980s signed, as sovereign states, a Compact of Free Association with the US. I was appointed non-resident Ambassador to all three island countries. It was necessary to tread warily on visits there given New Zealand's non-nuclear policy and the prominence of US security interests, especially in the Marshalls, which provided the premium site for American intercontinental missile testing and had earlier provided the testing ground at Bikini Atoll for 23 US atmospheric nuclear bomb experiments, the aftermath of which remained highly controversial. Prime Minister David Lange had emphasised New Zealand policy was 'not for export', but in all three countries it quickly became apparent many politicians and others were predisposed in New Zealand's favour; Palau even had non-nuclear policy inscribed in its constitution. In all three capitals support for the New Zealand policy was readily forthcoming and sometimes expressed purposefully in the presence of impassive US diplomatic representatives.

This beefed up New Zealand effort was all very well. But nothing could disguise the fact that the South Pacific experienced a roller coaster of domestic political misadventure during the second half of the 1980s. Two coups in Fiji in fairly rapid succession, engineered by the military under Colonel Sitiveni Rabuka with a decidedly racial complexion, overthrew a democratically elected government. Insurrection in Vanuatu – including threats against New Zealand's newly minted diplomatic presence in the capital, Vila – drove the government there to request New Zealand assistance.

At the same time in Papua New Guinea, secessionist conflict in Bougainville was costing many lives and there was increasing likelihood that New Zealand would be implicated as a conciliator, since those embroiled on the ground deemed Australia to be unacceptable for such a role. In New Caledonia, under French tutelage, Jean-Marie Tjibaou, the leader of the pro-independence movement Front de Libération Nationale Kanak et Socialiste (FLNKS), was assassinated, throwing into question the French Government's commitment there to a referendum about full independence. The so-called Matignon Accords, signed in 1988, deferred the referendum for ten years and some South Pacific Forum governments remained leery about France's intentions.

I accompanied Deputy PM Geoffrey Palmer to the Tjibaou funeral. Big crowds of indigenous Kanaks lined the streets of Nouméa, while the European French (Caldoche) took the opportunity of the funeral recess to flock to Nouméa's attractive beaches. The service at Saint Joseph's Cathedral was an import from a very different world. The Kanak choir sang in Latin, and there was plenty of organ music and incense. The French PM Michel Rocard was present with a squad of minders. At a subsequent 40-minute meeting with Geoffrey Palmer, Rocard – cool, dapper, engaging and speaking excellent English – admitted Paris had behaved unjustly over the *Rainbow Warrior* affair. He described the Tjibaou killing as a tragedy, and reaffirmed France's determination to stick by the Matignon Accords. Palmer queried why the French settler community had been so conspicuous by their absence from the funeral. Rocard was blindsided by the question; it had clearly not been a subject of discussion beforehand with his own acolytes. He muttered merely that Nouméa was after all a 'European town'. Palmer observed pertinently that perhaps France needed New Zealand and South Pacific understanding more than ever.

New Zealand's own attitude to France was conflicted by the *Rainbow Warrior* affair and persistent nuclear testing in French Polynesia (there were 25 such tests over the second part of the 1980s). New Zealand's response to *Rainbow Warrior* had, as noted earlier, produced accusations that Wellington was indeed bent upon 'chasing France from the South Pacific'. France was much discomfited too by a successful New Zealand-led 1986 campaign to reinscribe New Caledonia on the UN's list of colonial territories.

೧೩

The first Rabuka coup in Fiji in May 1987 caught New Zealand and its diplomats completely off guard. New Zealand's initial reactions, it would be true to say, were innocent of much forethought. David Lange, as Foreign Minister, revelled in masterminding (although that is not quite the right description) the New Zealand response. I was part of the crisis management team that spent time on the ninth floor of the Beehive with David Lange.

The PM cut corners, sweeping up the telephone frequently to speak directly with the New Zealand High Commissioner Rod Gates in Suva, with the Australian PM Bob Hawke in Canberra, with the Commonwealth Secretariat in London, and with politically engaged Indo-Fijian lawyers who were acquaintances from his legal days. It was a challenge at times to detect coherence in some of this, but subsequent criticism of David Lange for brinkmanship, in the matter of sending in New Zealand military to overturn the coup, was off the mark. His reactions needed to be weighed too against the complete failure of New Zealand officialdom in Wellington and Suva to anticipate the coup.

There were, not surprisingly, different shades of opinion and judgement amongst advisers about a suitable New Zealand response to these events. There was activism and prudence. There were doves and hawks. Some felt New Zealand had to 'do something' since the coup could not be allowed to stand and a quick robust New Zealand response was called for; others by contrast, judged New Zealand should be pragmatic ('what is done is done') and swing back to support Ratu Mara, Fiji's revered elder statesman, whose government had been defeated by the left-leaning Indo-Fijian leader Timoci Bavadra in the recent general election. That was the direct cause of the problem. The military coup led by Colonel Rabuka was aimed at protection of indigenous Fijian ascendancy. It was not clear whether Ratu Mara had prior knowledge of Rabuka's intentions, but there were suspicions. Lange, for his part, publicly condemned Ratu Mara for treachery just four days later, and branded Rabuka a usurper.

Once the initial shock had been digested in Wellington there was agreement New Zealand should openly express support for the Fijian Governor-General Penaia Ganilau as the rightful 'constitutional authority' for restoring legitimacy in Fiji, and Rod Gates in Suva was instructed to remain in closest touch. There were uncertainties about the Governor-General's resolve (the Queen sent him a strengthening message, the New Zealand Governor-General Sir Paul Reeves telephoned encouragement to his Fijian counterpart, and MERT backed a visit by ex-Governor-General Sir David Beattie for a peer-level heart-to-heart). The temperature then sharpened with a six-hour hijack of an Air New Zealand Boeing at Nadi Airport five days after the coup, which was resolved when the hijacker was bludgeoned with a full whisky bottle. Reported riots in Suva two days later added to the tension.

Rumours and speculation spread that a New Zealand military intervention to restore the situation was in the wind. As a member of the crisis management team I was aware that the New Zealand frigate HMNZS *Wellington*, which had coincidentally been off the coast of Fiji, was to remain 'over the horizon', and that an RNZAF C-130 Hercules had been placed on standby for the specific purpose of evacuating New Zealanders, but a military intervention intended to negate the coup was never envisaged. At a press conference on the day before the hijacking Lange ruled out New Zealand military intervention; and a week later he told members of the deposed Bavadra's government that New Zealand would not be part of any peacekeeping operation in Fiji, nor would it officially impose economic sanctions.

An authoritative New Zealand account (at least in the public domain) of the unfolding and confusing proceedings at the time remains to be written. Rabuka's unconstitutional assertion of the rights and interests of Fiji's indigenous people was acutely relevant to and for New Zealand. Prudence suggested New Zealand should 'hasten slowly' on the diplomatic front. Indeed, just four months later Colonel Rabuka launched a second coup, on the grounds that the objectives of the the original had not been met. He then arrested Timoci Bavadra and declared Fiji a republic. It was a febrile situation and it was not the end of the game. More illegal action was brewing. Between 1987 and 2007 a total of four Fijian coups d'etat were launched, not all driven by the same motives, but it is a singular record even by world standards.

Just how did other Pacific Islands' governments regard Colonel Rabuka's felony? I accompanied Prime Minister David Lange, two weeks after the first coup, to the annual Heads of Government South Pacific Forum meeting in Apia, where Fiji (who was not represented) was the ghost at the feast. At a closed-door meeting from which advisers were excluded, it soon became clear that Island leaders were not united by a sense of moral outrage at what had occurred in Fiji.

Leaders agreed to express anguish and concern over what had occurred, but acknowledged the complexity of the issue, and were ready to communicate to the Fijians that the Forum, through the Samoan chair, was willing to assist in any way the Fijian Governor-General (as the constitutional authority) thought appropriate. By deft drafting of the communiqué the leaders sidestepped an offer from Australian PM Bob Hawke to lead a mission to Fiji, which some leaders clearly considered might prove an exercise in grandstanding.

A Commonwealth Heads of Government (HOG) meeting in Vancouver very soon afterwards signalled that Fiji's membership had lapsed. The Fijian Governor-General now became republican Head of State and appointed Ratu Mara as Prime Minister, who would govern by decree. Mara shortly thereafter issued a statement calling upon South Pacific leaders to support him in restoring democracy.

New Zealand had in the interim itself held a general election (August 1987) which returned the Lange Government to office. The Prime Minister then divested himself of the foreign affairs portfolio and installed Russell Marshall as minister. The new minister did not carry quite the same weight politically, nor corporally, but was favourably disposed to indicate support for Ratu Mara's efforts. He made an early first telephone contact with the Fijian leader informing him New Zealand would like to resume its aid programme in Fiji, which had been suspended after the first coup. Marshall then accompanied Deputy PM Geoffrey Palmer to the 1988 South Pacific Forum in Tonga, where I was a delegation member. They met privately with Ratu Mara on the margins of that meeting, at which Fiji was again not represented.

All official New Zealand ministerial dealings with Fiji had ceased after the first coup. I was deputed to represent Trade Minister Mike Moore in early 1989 at a meeting of the Fiji/New Zealand Businessmen's Council. It was the first 'official' contact and chiefly notable for the fact that some 90 per cent of the Fijian participants were either Indian or European. That seemed to capture an essential problem in Fiji – the absence of an indigenous stake in the business economy.

I met Colonel Rabuka in early 1990 at the Suva Barracks, in company with John Henderson from David Lange's office and Royal New Zealand Navy (RNZN) Commodore Karl Moen. He was calm, measured and eloquent in expression of his desire for resumption of military cooperation with New Zealand. It was a polished performance. In another meeting, with Prime Minister Ratu Mara and the Pacific Policy Review Group from New Zealand, he affirmed indigenous Fijian paramountcy as the absolute governing principle for future politics in the country, while expressing a hope for better relations with New Zealand. It was a performance wise in its own conceit.

New Zealand's cup was running over elsewhere. In Vanuatu in mid-May 1988, renegade politician Barak Sopé led a march into the capital Vila, causing a riot with deaths, for the purpose of overthrowing the government of Prime Minister Walter Lini. The rupture was about land and political power. The Australians considered Sopé to be a pawn of Libya; their intelligence services suggested that Libya was taking unhealthy interest in the South Pacific. New Zealand had only just opened its diplomatic mission in Vila and our brand new High Commissioner Tony Browne found himself immediately confronted with a request from Prime Minister Walter Lini for New Zealand help with anti-riot gear, and a proposal that New Zealand place military forces on standby as a precaution.

Crisis management at the Prime Minister's Office on the ninth floor of the Beehive once more swung into action, which confirmed that even while we had a new Foreign Minister in Russell Marshall, David Lange retained the driving seat. The Domestic and External Security Committee chaired by Gerald Hensley was convened and strove to maintain a correct sense of proportion. It concluded New Zealand should entertain a direct request for combat military help only from a properly constituted authority inside Vanuatu, and only if there was an identified terrorist threat.

Confronted by this second regional emergency, the Australians had moved quickly to action stations. As mentioned, intelligence sources which indicated Libyan meddling in Vanuatu had already alarmed Canberra, and Foreign Minister Hayden had made a special trans-Tasman crossing to Ohakea a fortnight earlier, to brief David Lange. Canberra seemed prepared to intervene to remove Sopé. Things were serious.

The Fiji coup experience did help condition Wellington proficiency. An RNZAF C-130 departed for Vanuatu with gear and policemen in the early evening of the day of Lini's appeal. A second flight was despatched two days later. The Ministry's South Pacific directorate under Peter Bennett performed admirably. Closest contact was initiated and maintained with Australia (Russell Marshall called Australian Prime Minister Hawke) and the Domestic and External Security Committee agreed a contingency plan be drawn up with the Australians for joint military intervention, if required, operating out of Queensland.

The Ministry's advice to the government about the Vanuatu crisis emphasised a need for New Zealand to keep other South Pacific governments informed of New Zealand thinking; and if push came to shove, to propose appropriate South Pacific involvement with action intended to restore legitimate authority in Vanuatu. On the face of it Australia seemed less concerned by those sorts of considerations. The complexities in Vanuatu's politics remained truly difficult to comprehend: the crisis suddenly subsided and Prime Minister Lini dismissed Sopé, although the contest simmered until Lini arrested the renegade towards the end of the year and the Vanuatu Supreme Court condemned Sopé's treasonable behaviour. Foreign Minister Russell Marshall went on Radio New Zealand to declare support for Lini.

By coincidence a round of the newly minted New Zealand political and security talks in Vila with the people of Vanuatu (Ni-Vanuatu) had earlier been scheduled. They went ahead and provided a platform for New Zealand engagement at this sensitive time. One point of connexion between New Zealand and Vanuatu was that both had signed fisheries agreements with the Soviet Union. New Zealand and Vanuatu were actually the only two South Pacific governments with such an agreement; the Australians and Americans harboured suspicions about Soviet activity and therefore had no such common ground. The consultations in Vila demonstrated that regularised meetings with Pacific nations on issues of common interest gave New Zealand a comparative advantage during a sensitive period.

Throughout this time there was some discernible evidence of pushback on the part of South Pacific Island governments against New Zealand and Australian presumptions. One particular irritant which began to manifest itself in the 1980s was the predisposition amongst Australian and New Zealand diplomats for pre-cooking the annual Forum Leaders' communiqués in ways that privileged trans-Tasman interests and priorities. Moreover, Pacific governments had been directly encouraged, from Wellington and Canberra, to pursue membership in international institutions. The process widened horizons, fostered new associations beyond the region and consolidated aptitudes for international diplomacy (particularly on the part of Fiji and Papua New Guinea). Present generation activity by South Pacific Island governments on the critical issue of climate change amply confirms that aptitude.

In the present generation an increasingly confident China pursues ties with Pacific Island governments. New Zealand is committed meanwhile to 'reset' its relationships in the region, but if that entails greater readiness to 'choose friends' for South Pacific governments, New Zealand needs to tread very softly. This may not be easy if major powers and their principal allies insist upon defining the South Pacific simplistically as contested space between competing great powers, who therefore get to choose congenial partners for the islands' governments. New Zealand retains clear and real interests in the South Pacific, but employing 'big power' justification for its policies collides with its comparative advantage in the region, which lies in the ability to 'think small'.

In the 1980s Pacific Island governments engaged increasingly in caucusing amongst themselves. The Melanesians (Papua New Guinea, Solomons, Vanuatu, Fiji) decided in 1988 to establish the Melanesian Spearhead Group (MSG), whose ostensible purpose was to assert support for New Caledonian (Melanesian) independence from France. Whatever the precise motive, the MSG supplied Fiji with an alternative platform (although internal divisions subsequently plagued the grouping), while more generally it dispersed the foundations of regional cooperation. Likewise, proposals emerged for a Polynesian sub-regional grouping, promoted in particular from French Polynesia and its opportunistic leader Gaston Flosse, which envisaged exclusion of New Zealand and Australia. The King of Tonga, for one, appeared receptive to those siren calls at the time.

∽

Navigation of the trans-Tasman relationship with Australia was a paramount part of my role as Assistant Secretary at this time. The Australian Government had made clear their deep aversion to the New Zealand non-nuclear policy and the rift it had caused in the 1951 ANZUS security alliance. The American decision to suspend New Zealand from the alliance occurred two days before I took up my new Wellington responsibility in July 1986, and participating in the formulation of policy recommendations for New Zealand ministers, post-ANZUS in respect to Australia, was a priority. The New Zealand High Commissioner in Canberra, Graham Ansell, who was soon selected as the next permanent head of the Ministry in Wellington, was the point man of this New Zealand endeavour.

As mentioned earlier, both Australia and New Zealand had reviews of their respective defence policies (White Papers) coincidentally scheduled in 1986. The New Zealand document, still in draft, called for a future of strengthened defence ties with Australia in the wake of the ANZUS rift with America. However, the Australian Foreign Minister Bill Hayden, on a first visit to Wellington in December 1986, delivered the pungent message that New Zealand could not simply view Australia as a substitute protector after America's retraction. The ANZUS break was deeply regrettable, he said, and it was imperative that New Zealand now spend more on defence.

Astringency hung over the visit and disquieted David Lange. In the official exchanges with Hayden little was actually said on defence spending. Officials on both sides concurred that Hayden should be persuaded on his departure to express slightly more benevolent opinions about New Zealand, which he did at Auckland Airport. But the tone of the visit was captured by a boat trip at the Bay of Islands, where Hayden, in dark suit and tie and accompanied by similarly bedecked minders, arrived at the wharf to be greeted by Lange sporting voluminous beachwear for a programmed day's fishing. In the circumstances it seemed better to dispense with all thoughts of fishing and confine the day to a boat ride in pleasant surroundings.

The review of New Zealand defence policy was a singular exercise. It was led not by specialists in security and defence matters, but by John Henderson, head of the PM's advisory group and director of the Office of the Prime Minister. He was an academic, handpicked by David Lange, and had no background in Wellington officialdom. He had replaced the esteemed Gerald Hensley and it would be fair to say that they were very different personalities. Amongst government officials, including in the newly named MERT and among uniformed and non-uniformed defence personnel, there were observable hesitations about Henderson. He was, after all, 'not one of us'.

I worked quite closely and travelled extensively over four years with John Henderson, particularly in relation to the Defence White Paper and its implementation, as well as on the study of New Zealand South Pacific policy ('Towards a Pacific Islands Community', mentioned above) which he chaired; and for which he asked me to write the political chapters. We both attended South Pacific Forum meetings in company with David Lange, as well as discussions with Australians and with Americans in Washington. I learnt a good deal – above all that John Henderson was a person of principle.

The New Zealand Defence White Paper published in early 1987 was described as 'the most fundamental change in defence policy since World War Two'; it emphasised greater New Zealand self reliance in defence, principal focus on the South Pacific, and closer defence relations with Australia. There was nothing very novel in those priorities as such, but they were being restated in an entirely novel context, because of the rift with the US. The emphasis on greater New Zealand self reliance carried the direct implication that the post-ANZUS New Zealand defence budget would increase. Yet even as Cabinet signed off on the document there was no consensus amongst ministers that New Zealand should spend more on defence. Treasury, under their zealous minister Roger Douglas, was crusading for spending reductions right across the board.

A complication lay too in the uneasy relationship of the defence hierarchy, military and civilian, with their own disputatious minister Frank O'Flynn. It had reached the point where they were literally not talking to each other. By default MERT slipped into the vacuum, particularly over the thorny issue of the replacement of four ageing RNZN frigates, a big ticket item that became, in its turn, a particular touchstone for trans-Tasman relations. The Australian Defence White Paper had committed to an expansion of the Australian defence industry, and most particularly to the homegrown construction of eight new frigates for the Australian Navy.

It was no surprise when the Australians quickly calculated that adding four more vessels to the Australian build, to make up a round dozen, would enhance economies of scale and compatibility of equipment with New Zealand. Virile Australian powers of persuasion were brought to bear upon Wellington to 'buy Australian' when replacing the four existing New Zealand vessels. Such a decision would also fulfil New Zealand's declared objective of closer defence relations with Australia. Opportunities for New Zealand manufacturers to participate in the frigate build were dangled as an inducement; Prime Minister Bob Hawke, Defence Minister Kim Beazley, and a succession of officials and ship builders variously crossed the Tasman to apply pressure on decision makers. I was involved in much of this game of circles.

Real equivocation about the frigates nonetheless persisted amongst New Zealand ministers. Public opinion polls revealed rising non-government opposition in the street. The Labour Government's quirky arrangement of ministerial portfolios in the 1980s meant MERT found itself answerable to three ministers – Mike Moore, Russell Marshall and Fran Wilde. One was for the frigate project, one was opposed and one sat on the fence.

The Ministry's advocacy for the frigates, deriving from its place as watchdog of the trans-Tasman relationship, became a target of NGO disapproval. A particular occasion, amongst several, was a well attended conclave at Turnbull Library organised by the Chair of the Parliamentary Select Committee on Foreign Affairs, the much respected Sonja Davies, who was a trenchant opponent herself of the frigate project. Abandoning all thoughts of impartiality as chairperson, she joined in the chorus of denunciation of the proposed purchase from the floor. Commodore Woods and I, as advocates for the project, were treated to a sort of rowdy drumhead court martial. This was, I concluded privately, no place at all for officials. It should have been a politician's responsibility to withstand this heat.

Finally New Zealand ministers decided to acquire just two frigates from the Australian building programme. It was difficult to ignore the stridency of public opposition within New Zealand, which seemed to be as much anti-Australian as anti-frigate. For MERT, as custodian of the trans-Tasman relationship, this was problematic. Australian Defence Minister Kim Beazley explicitly called out the anti-Australianism. More than once on visits to New Zealand he had been greeted by placard-wielding protestors depicting him as Rambo, with shirt unbuttoned and a six-pack torso, offering warships.

At the time it was surprising to realise just how sparse were regularised ministerial discussions about political and security issues between New Zealand and Australian ministers and officials – apart from the opportunities provided by the regular trialogue of the ANZUS connexion, which was now a dead letter. New Zealand ministers agreed to suggestions from officials to raise the idea of regularised foreign minister exchanges with their Australian counterparts (the idea was tentatively inflated to also suggest regularised prime ministerial meetings). Australian officials proved distinctly lukewarm, unwilling to 'reward' New Zealand for dereliction of duty over ANZUS. New Zealand had to await the elevation of Gareth Evans as Australian Foreign Minister in September 1988 before the idea found favour. Evans proved supportive; and true to form then portrayed the idea as his own.

The celebration of Australia's bicentenary in 1988 was an opportunity for New Zealand to prove a point about the intrinsic worth of the trans-Tasman relationship. However, the choice of a suitable New Zealand gift to mark the event provided MERT with a headache because New Zealand ministers, and notably Mike Moore, could not agree on a suitable bequest from a list of submitted proposals. In the end a 19th century 12-metre yacht, the *Akarana*, built originally in Auckland and winner of the 1888 centenary regatta in Sydney, was selected. Roy Fergusson of the Ministry's Australia Division had found the decomposing hulk lying abandoned in a Sydney backwater. Beautifully restored by the RNZN, it seemed an ideal gift, although New Zealand ministers and the Chairman of the New Zealand Committee for the Australian Bicentenary (Michael Fay of America's Cup fame), with whom MERT was also required to work, were not of one mind about it.

The handover to Australian PM Bob Hawke took place on 20 August 1988, on a glorious summer afternoon on Sydney Harbour with many onlookers. The yacht was to be housed in the Australian National Maritime Museum, with a trust fund supplied to permit at least one outing per year on the harbour. I travelled with David Lange to the handover, which was preceded by prime ministerial talks in Canberra where the New Zealand team was one of the first foreign delegations to meet in the newly opened Australian parliamentary building – impressive in scale and design. Hawke predictably urged New Zealand to 'buy Australian' in the matter of frigates. Lange responded that four vessels would be too expensive, but two were on the cards.

In addition to the tricky defence agenda, the first five-year review of the 1983 Australia–New Zealand Closer Economic Relations Trade Agreement (ANCERTA, known in shorthand as CER) was due in 1988. Official-level negotiations had been proceeding (the head of MERT's Australia Division, Simon Murdoch, carried the Ministry's torch); they had concentrated upon accelerating free trade in merchandise goods, removing anti-dumping measures, harmonising business law and administrative practices, and widening the CER ambit to include free trade in services.

The 1987 New Zealand general election had intruded on proceedings, and differences about CER persisted on the New Zealand side. Treasury, on full throttle applying the rigour of Rogernomics, foresaw minimal advantage for that deregulation agenda from embellishment of CER. The Minister of Overseas Trade, Mike Moore, preferred to meld CER with the 1980 South Pacific Regional Trade and Economic Cooperation Agreement, and extend CER to Canada. Those ideas were simply a distraction from trans-Tasman business immediately to hand.

Commemoration of Australia's bicentenary also provided a headline opportunity for the two prime ministers to profess a 'visionary' Joint Prime Ministerial Statement about the trans-Tasman economic future, and sign off on agreements (reached at official level) in those areas mentioned. Last-minute New Zealand efforts to inject greater 'vision' into the Joint Prime Ministerial Statement saw Simon Murdoch and his Trade Department counterpart David Gamble detached from the 1988 Lange retinue in Sydney to engage with Australian counterparts in Canberra.

Overall the outcome did accelerate an advance towards the declared goal of a single market. It also signalled a new dimension by committing the governments to pursue scope for a trans-Tasman agreement on investment. Investment flows did not figure as a commonplace in trade agreements generally at that time, so there was some vision there. Australia undertook to cease industrial bounties and to open government purchasing contracts to New Zealand bidding. In purely practical terms New Zealand secured some gains, but in areas such as trade in dairy products Australian commitments fell short.

Aside from disagreements about non-nuclear policy, other differences, not of the same magnitude, coloured trans-Tasman dealings. Firstly, Australia pushed the candidature of former PM Malcolm Fraser for the position of Commonwealth Secretary-General. There were serious doubts in Wellington about his suitability, which had to be explained severally and diplomatically in Canberra.

Secondly, Australia walked away from a draft Convention on the Regulation of Antarctic Mineral Resource Activities, a New Zealand initiative (led by Chris Beeby) that had been under negotiation for seven years, and where Australia had been fully involved. At the eleventh hour, Australia pronounced the environmental protections insufficient and sided with France to favour instead an additional protocol on protections to be added to the Antarctic Treaty itself. Prime Minister Geoffrey Palmer decided, during a meeting with Bob Hawke in Auckland at which I was present, that New Zealand would follow suit.

Thirdly, the Australian Prime Minister strove to steal New Zealand thunder over the contentious practice of South Pacific drift-net fishing at the 1989 South Pacific Forum in Tarawa, Kiribati. New Zealand had been carrying the banner on drift-net fishing (alongside the US in the UN) and intended, as Australian officials knew, to highlight action on implementing a ban in the region, amongst the formal conclusions to be reached by the Pacific leaders at Tarawa. Prime Minister Hawke was now intent upon grabbing the banner; he signalled on arrival an Australian initiative on the issue. New Zealand leadership was only retrieved by swiftly offering to host a conference to negotiate a legal text to ban drift-net fishing in the region. Thanks to the energies of MERT's lawyers and its Pacific Division, this produced in short order the 1989 Wellington Convention for the Prohibition of Fishing with Long Drift Nets in the

South Pacific. The negotiations themselves created other opportunities: they attracted American State Department negotiators to Wellington – the first such visitors to New Zealand since the ANZUS bust up.

The 1989 Pacific Heads of Government Forum in Tarawa required a wrenching nine-hour flight by RNZAF C-130 Hercules for the New Zealand delegation led by David Lange. The capacious, spartan interior and the crescendo of engine noise (each passenger was equipped with large ear muffs) tested the staying power of the civilian bureaucrats as they pored uncomfortably over the briefing supplied by Wellington. The RNZAF had made special effort for the Prime Minister, in the form of a webbing hammock slung between bulkheads above the seating. David Lange availed himself of this 'extra'. The vision of his swinging bulky leadership presence gazing down on the heads of his delegation during the long thunderous hours of flight remains lodged in my mind.

Russell Marshall as Foreign Minister was also at Tarawa. He led for New Zealand in newly instituted Post Forum Dialogue with representatives from non-Pacific countries who were present as observers. Amongst them was the UK Minister of State for Foreign Affairs, Lord Glenarthur. He was a former army officer in the Royal Hussars, youthful, engaging and tailored in fine tropical clothing. The meeting took place in the modest residence of the British High Commissioner to Kiribati. Russell Marshall had immersed himself beforehand in South Pacific political details and the British Lord opened proceedings with 'I have come to learn'. Marshall began his tour of the Pacific horizon, speaking in his usual low gentle monotone. As he got into his stride it became suddenly apparent Glenarthur had elegantly fallen fast asleep and neither Marshall nor the British High Commissioner had noticed. Silent gesticulations to draw attention to the British Lord's slumber were needed to restore decorum. Ministerial somnolence at a face-to-face encounter like this was a first in my experience.

గ్ర

Staff turnovers in MERT at senior levels meant responsibility for oversight of the NZ–US relationship was landed in my lap as an additional duty at this time. The New Zealand Embassy in Washington, concerned always to demonstrate that New Zealand remained a worthwhile 'friend but not military ally' for the US, had floated ideas for official-level dialogue in Washington concentrated upon the South Pacific, at a time of some political upheaval within the region. The aim was to break ice with the Americans. They indicated a readiness on their part. The PM Geoffrey Palmer, who had himself personally experienced robust exchanges in Washington on New Zealand's non-nuclear policy, gave a green light. He summoned me to convey riding instructions.

In the normal course, New Zealand exchanges with government officials in Washington hardly merit a place in history, but given the state of NZ–US dealings at the time, they deserve a tiny footnote. We fielded a team drawn from the PM's Office (John Henderson), the Ministry of Defence, the External Assessments Bureau and the New Zealand Aid Programme. The New Zealand Ambassador Tim Francis and some of his staff joined in. The Americans, led by Deputy Assistant Secretary of State Marilyn Meyers, included officials from the Central Intelligence Agency, the Pentagon, the National Security Council and the Commerce Department. I called separately on Assistant Secretary of State Richard Solomon.

The exchanges were unremarkable. We explained various facets of New Zealand policy and a capacity to 'take pains' in the South Pacific, describing New Zealand policy as complementary to, not uniform with, Australian policy. Meyers pronounced the exchanges worthwhile, and suggested a repeat in a year or so. Calls were made separately on the Pentagon, as well as think tanks like the Heritage Foundation, which at that time exerted influence in the Reagan White House and where New Zealand non-nuclear policy was complete anathema. At the meeting, Heritage Foundation staffers conveyed the unmistakable impression that they were supping with the devil, or at least his representative.

Non-official contacts with Washington were also allowed. I was lucky in October 1987 to be offered a place by Georgetown University at a two-week leadership programme dedicated to discussion of 'political, economic and security systems in 2000'. I sought ministerial approval to attend. There were 25 participants drawn from a range of different countries. One of the two organisers was Professor Madeleine Albright, who became American Ambassador to the UN and then President Clinton's Secretary of State; and with whom I sat around the UN Security Council table in New York in my next incarnation.

Albright had put together an impressive range of top drawer Washington contributors – officials, academics, pundits and lobbyists – with contrasting and sometimes controversial opinions. One discussion with Michael McGuire, a reputable Senior Fellow at the liberal think tank the Brookings Institution, revealed that he was a rare species: a confirmed enthusiast in Washington for the New Zealand non-nuclear policy. There was enough curiosity at Georgetown University about the New Zealand policy that I was invited to lead a tutorial for a dozen or so post-graduates, drawn from America's European alliance partners, who were plainly unconvinced by New Zealand's delinquency.

All of the above coincided domestically with implementation across the entire New Zealand public service of the revolutionary 1988 State Sector Act, a signature policy of the New Zealand Labour Government. It involved fixed-term contracts (notably for chief executives), the flattening of structures, and the restructuring of responsibility and accountability, while promoting contestability and the outsourcing of advice. It heralded the age of public service 'managerialism', which I thought came at some cost for policy thinking within the newly christened (as part of the reforms) MERT. Furthermore a 'no surprises' rule of thumb, adopted in the 1990s for government departments when interacting with ministers, compounded problems for policy advice fearlessly given. It nourished risk aversion.

One early result of the reforms in MERT was suppression of the six Assistant Secretary positions within the Ministry. Job security in Wellington became an immediate concern. The MERT Secretary (now Chief Executive) Merv Norrish retired and was replaced by Graham Ansell, who immediately confronted the task of consolidating changes required by the reforms. I received offers of more than one overseas posting, but none of the initial suggestions were attractive, and I had spent less time in Wellington over recent years than most of my peers. Graham Ansell then offered me the post as New Zealand Permanent Representative to the UN in New York, because the incumbent, Anne Hercus, wished to return home for personal reasons. I was aware the posting had been offered to at least one other officer, who had declined. Elizabeth and I pondered and we accepted.

9. ON THE EAST RIVER

New York in the early 1990s offered the enticement of living in a place of immense exhilaration. My assignment there coincided with commemorations of the 500th anniversary of Christopher Columbus's arrival in America (a celebration not without controversy); with a Presidential election and the arrival of Bill Clinton in the White House; with distressing racial riots in Los Angeles sparked by the killing of Rodney King, a black American, which had repercussions in New York; and with the extraordinary siege and mass killing in Texas of members of the Branch Davidian religious sect.

It coincided too with events in the wider world which affected working life at the UN – the end of the 40-year Cold War between the US and the Soviet Union, the break up of the old Soviet Union, the disintegration of Yugoslavia, Iraq's invasion of Kuwait, the reunification of Germany, and the resignation of Margaret Thatcher in the UK, as well as the launch of the World Wide Web. On the New Zealand domestic front, 11 days after our arrival in New York Prime Minister Geoffrey Palmer resigned, and in a general election nine weeks later, a new National Party government led by Jim Bolger defeated the short-lived Labour administration of Mike Moore.

Our accommodation at East 84th Street and East End Avenue in upper Manhattan was a comfortable duplex apartment, originally acquired by PM Keith Holyoake as the New Zealand residence. Built in the 1920s–30s, the block was not high rise by New York standards. It stood on Gracie Square, adjacent to the attractive wooden 18th century official residence of the mayor of New York. A succession of New Zealand ambassadors had enjoyed the premises, which overlooked the East River, Roosevelt Island and the flow of the constant riverborne

131

traffic. It was some 40 blocks from the New Zealand Mission office and the UN Building, and it took just over 40 minutes on foot (computed on the rough New York walking rule of one minute per block) to reach the office. That walk provided a daily constitutional along the East River (in parallel with Roosevelt Drive) winter and summer.

New Zealand's involvements with the UN in New York a whole generation ago hardly warrant detailed recollection here. The day-to-day grind of yesterday's so-called multilateral diplomacy would, in the telling, provide a guaranteed cure for insomnia. There were two main preoccupations. First was preparation for, and participation at, the Rio Environment Summit in Brazil, which turned out to be the largest assembly of world leaders in history but which did not include New Zealand's leader – and thereby hangs a tale.

Second was the campaign to win a two-year (1993/94) New Zealand seat on the UN Security Council, against stiff competition, after an absence of 40 years since the previous two-year term (1953/54). New Zealand had also experienced a one-year stint in 1966 that was essentially an honorific gesture by major powers towards New Zealand at the moment when Council membership was being enlarged to 15 members. None of those previous tenures were contested and there had been no serious campaigning required to obtain a place.

New Zealand's first taste of competitive bidding for a Council seat occurred in 1980, in competition with Malta. It produced an infamous defeat on the floor of the UN General Assembly as African governments, to a man, blackballed New Zealand because of its sporting contacts with apartheid South Africa. It was the diplomatic equivalent to the sporting boycott of the 1976 Montreal Olympic Games by African nations for precisely the same reason. Those were not famous years for New Zealand's international reputation.

The need to avoid failure this time around was therefore plain to be seen. I undertook to New Zealand ministers that if at any time during the campaign the New Zealand Mission sensed another defeat (and the competition was indeed strong), we would immediately recommend withdrawal, even at the eleventh hour.

Every New Zealand Ambassador and High Commissioner receives from the New Zealand Foreign Minister a letter of appointment, setting out the duration, objectives and priorities for their assignment. My New

York letter, signed out by Mike Moore, was curiously silent in some respects. It made no mention of the duration of the posting, nor did it mention anything about responsibility for leading the New Zealand official delegation at the scheduled 1992 Rio Environment Summit and its extensive preparatory conferences, despite the Summit being the headline event looming on the global economic and social agenda. (A message did indeed soon arrive in New York commissioning me with the task, which proved very demanding.) But most of all the letter was silent about the pursuit of New Zealand's candidature for a 1993/94 seat on the UN Security Council (UNSC). The bid had lain upon the table at the UN for a matter of years, and the time for doing something serious about it was fast approaching. It was possible to surmise the reasons for the omission – but the first thing was to clear up the duration for my assignment. I sought clarification from the senior officer responsible for composing the letter of instruction, my colleague Colin Keating, who confirmed by way of a 'note for file' that the appointment was for four years.

The letter's silence about the UNSC bid could possibly be explained by the immediate context in Wellington. It is not an overstatement to recall that there was distinct equivocation amongst senior Ministry policy advisers about the whole venture. Indeed, I later learnt, the Ministry had twice recommended withdrawal of the New Zealand bid. The candidature had been discussed severally around the Policy Board table in head office, where I had participated, but well before any notion that I might actually be the UN Ambassador. Hesitancy was plain. Some colleagues believed New Zealand simply could not succeed; some that New Zealand's irrefutable external priority remained trade liberalisation (at the concurrent Uruguay Round of trade negotiations in Geneva) and, in the words of one very senior officer, Security Council membership would 'butter no parsnips' for New Zealand; others were concerned lest a seat on the Council would compound difficulties for New Zealand's relations with the US – bedevilled as they were by the stand-off over New Zealand's non-nuclear policy. On the very eve of the actual 1992 vote in New York (so I was told later) one senior officer pronounced New Zealand interests would be best served the next day by 'an elegant loss'.

In all of this coincidence was a factor. With a general election imminent in 1990 and every sign of a Labour government defeat, some

Ministry colleagues anticipated (hoped?) a new National government might set aside the Council bid as an extravagance, just as they also anticipated possible reversal of the non-nuclear policy were National to win office. The Ministry's own on-line potted history about the period concedes there were 'long faces' about the non-nuclear policy amongst advisers.

However during a 1990 call upon the Opposition Leader Jim Bolger before I left for New York, he made it very clear to me that, if or when elected, his government would sturdily pursue and succeed with the Security Council bid. He had by then also signalled publicly that a National government would not overturn the Labour policy concerning US Navy ship visits. That was confirmed in March 1990 by the National Party caucus, which in its turn had led to the resignation in protest by Don McKinnon as National Party spokesman for foreign affairs. Don McKinnon was destined very soon after National's electoral victory to take up the portfolio of Foreign Minister, with oversight of the UNSC campaign. Not so gentle irony intruded whenever he encountered (for example, when I accompanied him around the traps in New York) warm compliments from other ministers and ambassadors about New Zealand's non-nuclear policy, which preceded assurances of support for New Zealand's Security Council ambitions.

Whatever the ambivalence about the Security Council bid amongst the Ministry leadership in Wellington, at the operational level inside the Ministry, in the United Nations Directorate (under Tony Small) there were no compunctions. There was acute realisation that our competition for the two available seats was tough: Sweden, Spain and Turkey (Turkey eventually withdrew). Exchanges between the Directorate and the New York Mission included a request for ideas for a campaign blueprint (given the undistinguished failure in 1980 there was no 'how to win' New Zealand master plan). A blueprint was proposed by the Mission and then tweaked in some particulars by Wellington. It was adapted 20 years later as the basis for New Zealand's successful bid for a third two-year term on the 2014/15 Security Council; however, considerably greater financial and staff resources were devoted to that cause.

Basically the Security Council campaign trek lasted 18 months, involving three phases: an initial burst in New York canvassing all or most of the 194 delegations; a second phase of hard slog petitioning for support around capitals and on the margins of international conferences by ministers, special representatives and government officials; and a third phase where the spotlight was refocussed on New York. It was pretty clear on the ground that in a tight race for Security Council membership between three countries (each estimable in their own way), many governments when instructing their New York missions would cut their representatives some slack about where finally to place their vote, particularly if more than one ballot was required. So it proved.

CR

Preparations for the competing attraction of the Rio Environment Summit, scheduled for June 1992, consumed many months, with multiple meetings (official and non-official) in and around New York, as well as Geneva – some spread out over weeks. The Rio Summit was just the third meeting of its kind. It proved an immense jamboree. Of the 172 countries attending, 102 were represented by heads of state or government. It was at the time the largest head of government assembly in history, with some 8000 journalists and 2400 non-government organisations in attendance, as well as a large parallel NGO forum on the margins. Overall there were in excess of 20,000 participants involved at or around the meeting, which lasted 11 days.

At Rio and during the preparatory meetings, the extensive agenda up for negotiation meant there could be as many as 20 separate negotiating groups, beavering away simultaneously, that participating delegations had to cover. Keeping a finger on the pulse, let alone coordinating the overall New Zealand effort, was a test. The size of the New Zealand delegation grew like topsy throughout the process; at the first preparatory meeting it comprised eight members, 22 at the second, 25 at the third, and at Rio itself there were 22, including politicians like Geoffrey Palmer, David Caygill, Nick Smith and Peter Dunne, plus the Māori Congress led by the Māori Queen, Te Arikinui Dame Te Atairangikaahu. Throughout the preparation, New Zealand delegation members worked heroically over long hours and sleepless nights. Needless to say all this generated a blizzard of messages reporting back to home base; at the end of the last preparatory session in New York, for example, the New Zealand delegation despatched 27 lengthy telegrams back to Wellington outlining progress across different issues, and seeking further instruction.

When appointed as leader of the New Zealand officials delegation, I had little inkling from distant New York of the extent to which differences persisted in Wellington, amongst government advisers, about desirable policy directions. Close study of briefings supplied by Wellington did not always reveal the extent to which differences of view had been papered over in the briefing documents. But the differences became quickly clear in the continuous internal huddles of the New Zealand delegation throughout the lengthy preparation stages and at Rio.

The basic conundrum for New Zealand (and for everyone else) was devising common action for global environmental protection and sustainable development, when most governments had yet to decide coherent domestic policies. The aim at Rio was to reach collective agreement on a grand bargain in the form of Agenda 21, an extensively negotiated document comprising some 40 separate sector chapters, which delineated the foundations for environmental and sustainable best practice. Each chapter involved intricate negotiation. A Declaration of Principles was also to be negotiated and passed by the Summit to guide governments in their policy formulation.

The process had lapsed quickly and predictably into the classical developed versus developing country zero-sum game of winners and losers. The developing countries asserted that environmental dangers were the product of developed country industrialisation and intensified production practices, and therefore developed countries bore major responsibility to mitigate and remove the consequential environmental damage (and commit copious additional financial resources to that end). For their part, the developed countries took the view that environmental damage was universally harmful and all countries must commit to sharing the burden of mitigation. Major powers made plain they would never accept specified targets to reduce their environmental damage.

The New Zealand delegation's instructions were clear. We should keep our head below the parapet even as we strove to promote and protect specific interests – for example, acceptance by the conference that New Zealand forestry development practices provided a contribution to the mitigation of carbon emissions (David Payton of MERT worked strenuously and successfully here). But we were adamantly instructed to avoid giving any impression whatsoever that New Zealand was in a position to trade off offers of 'new and additional' aid finance as part of the Rio outcome. This cramped New Zealand's ability to work with 'like-minded' delegations such as Canada, who sought to abridge conference language, but not flatly deny the need for 'new and additional' resources. Towards the end of proceedings, in response to New Zealand delegation pleading, Wellington agreed to ease somewhat its adamant stand on language.

Canada was the important player throughout because the chief organiser of the whole Rio Summit production, retained as a consultant by the UN Secretariat, was a Canadian, Maurice Strong. He was an energetic oil and minerals businessman, accustomed to mixing in high political circles. He had visited Wellington in order to engage Prime Minister Jim Bolger's interest and convince him to participate at Rio. In conversations with Strong in New York and Geneva, he urged upon me that there would be a vital need throughout the process for mediators and conciliators, particularly at the culmination in Rio, and that a New Zealand leader would be one obvious candidate. As the Summit loomed I was surprised to be instructed then to convey the news that the Prime Minister would not now attend Rio, as domestic imperatives took precedence. It visibly disappointed Strong, and also the Brazilians, who by way of response tweaked the New Zealand nose.

Instead the New Zealand delegation leader was Rob Storey, Minister of Transport and formerly President of Federated Farmers. He was ranked sixteenth in the Bolger Cabinet and had little direct involvement with New Zealand environmental policy. He brought to Rio as his chief adviser the CEO of the Ministry for the Environment, Roger Blakeley, and he and I shared the position of deputy Summit delegation leader.

Amidst all the captains and kings at Rio, this level of New Zealand political representation was niggardly (all ten Pacific Islands delegations, for example, were led by heads of government). As a result New Zealand's delegation leader was not implicated in top-level horse trading, nor invited to the various celebrations where the notables communed (involving presidents like Bush, Mitterand and Castro, plus a big cast of prime ministers). Members of the New Zealand delegation, including Rob Storey, strove nevertheless to compensate through industrious engagement in the official-level negotiations.

At the height of proceedings I was approached by the Brazilian Chief of Protocol, who informed me that even though New Zealand could not be associated with the scheduled presentation of a specially commissioned Rio Summit Leaders Momento to heads of state or government, the Brazilian authorities had decided to bestow one upon the Māori Queen at a separate presentation. The Brazilians were quite aware of potential New Zealand government sensitivities here. It was, however, a fait accompli. I immediately informed Rob Storey, who protested, but not to the Brazilians. He telephoned Wellington forthwith. At the New Zealand delegation meeting the next morning, Dame Te Atairangikaahu smilingly entered the room with her supporters, carrying the official Rio Summit Leaders Momento, which she placed wordlessly and reverently on the boardroom table. Storey was poker faced.

Rio was the first international conference where tangata whenua in the form of Māori Congress had been designated as full New Zealand delegation members; some Rio delegations included indigenous groups on their delegation lists, but only as consultants or advisers. In the Agenda 21 document negotiated at the Summit, chapter 26 concerns strengthening the role of indigenous people in environment and sustainable development. The chairman of that negotiating group sought me out at the conclusion of proceedings (which I did not personally attend) to record appreciation for the contribution by the New Zealand tangata whenua representatives, without whom agreement would not, he said, have been possible.

In the reporting cable to Wellington signed out by Rob Storey, this was duly noted and the Summit overall portrayed as neither a success nor a failure but an inescapable foundation to set in motion a global process, the success of which was hardly assured. It was in the very nature of the beast that throughout the Summit process and its lengthy preparations, there were real differences within the large New Zealand delegation. But for one reason or another they did not, in the end, constitute breaking points for actual New Zealand involvement on the key issues at the Summit.

CR

The New Zealand intention to win a two-year seat on the 1993/94 UNSC represented a substantial competing attraction with the Rio

Summit and its lengthy preparation. The lobbying in New York for the Council seat began in April 1991 and concluded by a vote at the UN General Assembly in October 1992, with New Zealand elected, on a second ballot, for a two-year term. It was only the second full two-year term for New Zealand since the United Nations' creation in 1945.

The campaign consumed my energies for 18 months. I calculated that by the end of it all I had had over 400 one-on-one meetings with ministers, ambassadors, and other notables pleading the New Zealand cause, including beyond New York in Ghana, Senegal and Indonesia (where I joined Foreign Minister Don McKinnon and New Zealand Ambassador Neil Walter on the margins of the big annual Non-Aligned Movement conference). It was a voyage of discovery, in the sense that one encountered views, impressions and opinions of New Zealand and New Zealanders from the politicians and diplomats of countries with whom, in the normal course, New Zealand had negligible or even non-existent dealings. Most people in the world had never met a New Zealander, and those that had would have met only one or two; yet their political deductions about the country were extensively amiable and in the end helped tip the balance.

My first meeting with Don McKinnon occurred in Washington in May 1991. He asked straight-out: could New Zealand win a Security Council seat in the 1992 vote? I answered that there was much water to pass under the bridge, but given a fair wind at our back and a share of luck, New Zealand could succeed. I was well aware of the scepticism in senior parts of the Ministry, and stressed therefore the need to display complete and sustained commitment to the cause, of the kind traditionally reserved for New Zealand trade access into Europe or in negotiation at Geneva, where I had first-hand experience. Signs of ambivalence in Wellington would be readily detected by foreign diplomatic missions there, I suggested. McKinnon instructed me to put it all down in writing for discussions on his return home, which I did.

Calculations, assessments and sheer guesswork about the progress and likely result of the campaign waxed and waned throughout the 18 months – New York and Wellington each kept a scorecard, and the two more or less coincided as we compared notes. It soon became clear in New York that favourable impressions left by distinguished predecessors as New Zealand Ambassadors to the UN certainly counted in our favour. Lobbying was pursued at all levels of New Zealand Mission activity. James Kember, Jane Coombs and Adele Mason performed heroically. The latter kept score of those 'for', 'against', 'undecided' and 'backsliding'. This was essential for sustained targeting. A paper trail of letters to those lobbied, expressing anticipated gratitude, stretched far. James Kember helped raise the New Zealand profile by persuading UN organisers to schedule PM Jim Bolger's address to the 1991 UN General Assembly immediately prior to that of US President George H. W. Bush, thus guaranteeing a packed house of leaders and notables.

No stone could be left unturned. Lobbying amongst the large swirl of African leaders in colourful national dress in Senegal, on the margins of an Organisation of African Unity (OAU) summit, Jane Coombs and I encountered three different gentlemen, each bearing the name tag 'Foreign Minister of Somaliland', whom we separately canvassed for their country's support (we learnt later the three were from different tribes, each competing for political supremacy inside their country). In addition we had our campaign literature translated into Arabic, Spanish and French and distributed it accordingly to all OAU ministers, as well as throughout diplomatic missions in New York.

ଔ

Prime ministerial lobbying provided the icing on the campaign cake. Jim Bolger came to New York for the UN General Assembly sessions in 1991 and in 1992 where, thanks to ardent corridor arrangements by the New Zealand Mission, he was able to buttonhole a whole selection of prime ministers and foreign ministers to good effect. After each encounter a letter was sent under his signature, welcoming the opportunity to put the case and record (sometimes with tongue in cheek) the encouragement he had received.

At the 1991 Commonwealth Heads of Government Meeting in Harare, Zimbabwe, the Prime Minister secured assurances of support from the assembled leaders, including the UK. When I told the British UN Ambassador David Hannay, he was nonplussed. Hitherto he had loftily dismissed entreaties in New York for British support by remarking that it was far too early for Her Majesty's Government to decide. It did, however, become clear later that not all Commonwealth governments, when push came to shove, had stuck by assurances readily given to New Zealand at Harare.

For New Zealand the 1991 UN General Assembly session lived up to its reputation for providing the opportunity for leaders to commune privately and melt the ice. Prime Minister Bolger was seated with President Bush at the UN Secretary-General's lunch. They conversed and it was signalled later to the New Zealand Mission that President Bush was amenable to an informal meeting that evening with the New Zealand Prime Minister at the Waldorf Astoria Hotel on Park Avenue, at the conclusion of the President's traditional reception for UN delegates. That encounter on 23 September 1991 was the first by a New Zealand Prime Minister with the US President since 1984 and the rupture over New Zealand's non-nuclear policy. The huddle occurred in a side room off the Waldorf's main reception area, containing two armchairs and a sofa. The two leaders took refreshment in the form of a glass of whisky each, while Mrs Bolger was hosted by Barbara Bush in an alcove nearby.

Bolger left an account of the event in his 1998 biography *A View from the Top*. There were five people present: President Bush, his National Security Adviser Brent Scowcroft and a National Security staffer Doug Paal, and Prime Minister Jim Bolger, plus myself. The President was affable with a dignified light touch and slightly patrician air. He recalled his wartime experiences in the South Pacific and expressed an earnest wish for good relations in that part of the world. He recognised there was a problem with New Zealand over the non-nuclear policy, which he knew was supported by the majority of New Zealanders, but suggested there might be ways to 'ameliorate' US–NZ difficulties. He asked Scowcroft to elaborate.

The latter suggested enigmatically the US had certain 'big ideas' in the pipeline that could help move things along, but which could not be disclosed just yet. Bush added with a laugh that the US did not mean to sound too 'mysterious' about it all, but what did the Prime Minister think? There was here a cryptic (almost Monty Python-like) quality to proceedings. Mr Bolger was being asked informally to respond to ideas that could not be divulged even informally. The PM acknowledged the President's constructive approach and added that New Zealand was ready to listen to all American ideas, but domestic political realities were such that there could be no amendment to New Zealand nuclear legislation.

The meeting lasted about 25 minutes and broke up in good spirits. We cudgelled our brains afterwards about what the elliptical American 'big ideas' could possibly be. It was approaching midnight and we decided to sleep on it and convene an early morning meeting with the others of the Prime Minister's party, which included our Washington Ambassador Denis McLean. I telephoned MERT just to inform them that a meeting had occurred.

Next morning there was plenty of theorising about the meaning of it all, but the Prime Minister himself was not into theorising; to him the meeting was itself the achievement. The reporting message back to Wellington skipped our theories. Four days later, after the PM had left New York, there was a public announcement from Washington: the 'big ideas' were that henceforward the US would withdraw nuclear weapons from US Navy surface ships. The right to restore them in times of national security threat was reserved, and the 'neither confirm nor deny' policy governing their presence on board remained a basic precept; nevertheless it was a move in a direction more amenable to New Zealand.

ॐ

As the vote on the New Zealand Security Council bid approached, our attention turned to the nuts and bolts of the actual ballot itself. The statutory requirement for success would be support from two thirds of the UN members present and voting in the General Assembly. That meant each of the three candidates for the two seats available would need a minimum of 115 votes. In New York we calculated that it was almost impossible, in a three-way contest, for two of the candidates to each muster 115 votes in an initial ballot. It was likely that one of the trio would secure the requisite votes, and the other two would then have to fight it out in a second ballot. Thus it proved.

A second ballot strategy needed to be devised as a precaution. We decided the best approach would be importunate lobbying right up to the very last moment on the floor of the General Assembly. We would target a group of selected delegations, principally from Latin America, to vote for New Zealand on a second ballot even if they had not voted in our favour in round one (when each delegation had been entitled to two votes because there were two vacancies) – always providing New Zealand did well enough on that first ballot. Such petitioning required 'working the room' even as the Chairman gavelled the meeting for a second ballot.

It paid off. On the first ballot Spain was elected (118 votes), with New Zealand and Sweden level pegging, but below the two-thirds threshold (Sweden 109 and New Zealand 108). On the second ballot our ploy worked by effectively peeling away some 30-odd votes from Sweden, who, confident of success, had no backup plan. A third ballot was a formality to push New Zealand above the two-thirds requirement. The whole experience was a piece of sheer theatre.

Post-mortems were plenty. Voting was of course secret. One could never be absolutely certain of the way others had finally recorded their ballot. But one factor stuck out. New Zealand did not owe success to the Western governments in whose electoral group at the UN New Zealand incongruously belonged, and remains. The majority in that group favoured our competition. New Zealand was elected in effect by the rest of the world – Asia, Africa and Latin America, as well as the South Pacific, whose representatives agreed beforehand to cast their vote strategically in order to benefit New Zealand. The New Zealand non-nuclear policy influenced the extent of the support in both groups to an appreciable degree.

All of that obviously had to have an influence upon New Zealand's actual role as a Security Council member. In its post mortem cabled report the New Zealand Mission registered that point with Wellington. The Foreign Minister Don McKinnon had himself chosen rather to portray the successful outcome publicly as a signal that New Zealand had now regained a place on the 'first fifteen' as part of the 'western alliance'. However it was portrayed, it was clear that earlier fears in Wellington amongst some politicians and senior advisers that New Zealand had somehow lost its way internationally because of the non-nuclear policy had been emphatically disproven by our Security Council success.

That 'New Zealand lost' claim was equally confounded over the decade that followed, when under different governments New Zealand notched up a series of accomplishments: successful candidatures for Mike Moore and Don McKinnon for leadership roles in the WTO

and the Commonwealth Secretariat, respectively; a key role in pursuit
of a World Court case on nuclear weapons in The Hague; selection of
Kenneth Keith as the first New Zealander to become a judge at the World
Court; and hosting the Commonwealth Heads of Government Meeting
(CHOGM) in 1995 and the Asia-Pacific Economic Cooperation (APEC)
Leaders Summit in 1999, which brought a UK Prime Minister (John
Major) and a US President (Bill Clinton), respectively, to New Zealand
for only the second time since 1840. Meritorious peace support efforts
were also launched in Bosnia, Bougainville (where novel New Zealand
methods of reconciliation succeeded), East Timor and the Solomons.
And in the domain of trade policy, New Zealand began negotiations
with China for a free trade agreement, the first by a Western economy.
Not every New Zealand endeavour was crowned by success. But the
New Zealand scorecard overall, in the aftermath of the UN Security
Council success, refuted substantively the idea that nuclear-free New
Zealand was 'lost'.

☙

Amidst the intense tussle of the Security Council campaign, the duration
of my tour of duty in New York suddenly and unexpectedly became an
issue. Six months out from the actual vote on New Zealand's candidacy,
I was informed verbally by a senior Ministry colleague (at an airport as
boarding calls for his departure were sounding) that the Minister of
Foreign Affairs had decided that should New Zealand win the Security
Council seat, I would be replaced as New Zealand's UN Ambassador,
but should New Zealand miss out, then I could remain to serve out my
term of four years – due to end in the last quarter of 1994.

Changeover of New Zealand ambassadors is hardly a matter of
consequence in the normal scheme of things. It barely warrants even a
footnote in official history, and there is none in this instance. But this
was an unusual proposition at an unusual time, calculated to create
uncertainty during intense electioneering for a Security Council place.
When compared to practice by other UN members, a decision to change
ambassadors on the very threshold of entering the UN Security Council
would also be most unusual. So the tale merits a quick diversion here.

I had no knowledge of the precise reasons offered to Foreign Minister
Don McKinnon for the change. On the face of it the Ministry hierarchy

was setting aside a principle it traditionally applies when recommending all New Zealand Head of Mission appointments to government: that the nominee possesses qualifications sufficient for all foreseeable responsibilities involved during the term of the appointment (and in this case that included the UN Security Council). The change now envisaged was seemingly intended to 'improve' New Zealand performance on the Security Council.

The proposition that the changeover would only occur if New Zealand were to win, but not otherwise, suggested that somewhere in Wellington someone was 'writing their own ticket'. Whether true or not, there was a genuine question about how wise such a change would be. Experience of multilateral diplomacy as Head of Mission in New York, Geneva and Brussels had demonstrated to me that the truism of 'who you know and what you know' is notably important in multilateral diplomacy. Such knowledge takes time to acquire; the second ballot strategy devised in New York, which secured New Zealand's seat in the Security Council, bore witness to that.

More directly, as the lobbying for the Council seat intensified, responses from other UN ambassadors increasingly included a query of 'and who will actually represent New Zealand on the Council?' I had hitherto responded that my appointment to New York was for four years – through to the last quarter of 1994 – which would coincide pretty much with expiry of a New Zealand two-year term on the Council. I forewarned the hierarchy in Wellington that knowledge of New Zealand's intention for an eleventh hour change of ambassador could cost votes in what was clearly going to be a very tight competition. As a comeback I was advised to prevaricate whenever the question arose. That was, by most standards, perverse advice.

Contrived leaks subsequently appeared in the Wellington weekly newsletter *Trans Tasman* stating a change of UN Ambassador would occur 'when O'Brien's term ends' (which was not of course until late 1994). There was no leaked speculation about whether a changeover would damage New Zealand prospects in the vote, nor mention of the perverse condition attached to the changeover – if New Zealand did not succeed.

Our family arrangements had been made on the basis of a four-year assignment. Our two younger sons, Daniel and Timothy, were studying in New York, with important exams scheduled for mid-1993. The lease on our Wellington house had been made upon the same basis. After the prolonged intensity of the Security Council campaign, Elizabeth (who had materially helped carry the burden) and I now confronted the prospect of having to pack up in the space of a few weeks, although we could not be certain about it until the Security Council vote was decided, one way or another.

It is essential, although difficult, then and now, to always retain the right sense of proportion. The sky was not about to fall in; nonetheless I took the opportunity of Jim Bolger's attendance at the 1992 UN General Assembly (with the Security Council vote imminent) to raise my misgivings about the wisdom of the change, and the inconvenience it would cause to me and my family. If word got out beforehand about an imminent eleventh-hour New Zealand change of ambassador, our fortunes in the Security Council ballot could, I said, be compromised. He undertook to reflect and consult with others about the matter. Before he departed New York two days later, he informed me that after reconsideration, it had been agreed to proceed on the basis that a changeover would occur not from 1 January but from June 1993. It was a reprieve and I was grateful. But it was not a stay of execution.

☙

My firsthand Security Council experience was shortened and complex – it lasted six months. It was dominated by the discharge of the Presidency in March 1993, and by participation in a Security Council special mission to war-torn Bosnia in April 1993 – only the second mission of its kind in the Security Council's existence up to that point. An additional and uncongenial burden was chairmanship of the Security Council's Iraq Sanctions Committee, set up after the first Gulf War in 1990 to punish Iraq for its belligerence, which New Zealand was assigned by the five permanent members of the UNSC (US, UK, France, Russia and China), effectively with no prior consultation. This entailed close interaction with the UN Secretariat, regularised formal and informal Committee meetings, and corridor exchanges with the Iraqi UN Ambassador and visiting officials from Baghdad. It also involved fielding complaints severally from ambassadors of other countries that were being collaterally damaged by the Iraq sanctions.

It goes with the territory that New Zealand representatives overseas are often required to advance or defend New Zealand government policies about which they might retain personal and private doubts. Professionalism requires such doubts be set aside. The harsh sanctions against Iraq, however, were an agreed international response being enforced with such rigour that it produced deplorably inhumane consequences. The Iraqi leader Saddam Hussein was a tyrant who had undeniably inflicted great pain upon his people. But application of the international sanctions was critically flawed. The US opposed all imports into Iraq that represented 'inputs to industry' (cotton fabrics, glass, water pipes, irrigation equipment, medical refrigerators, vaccines and even, for a period, food). The doleful experience of the Sanctions Committee chairmanship was something I gladly relinquished.

Diplomacy in an interdependent world intensified as an exercise in networking. I was lucky that when New Zealand joined the Security Council in January 1993 I had personally encountered five of the 15 ambassadors around the UNSC table in previous incarnations – including three of the permanent Council members (UK, US and France). The British representative David Hannay, a confident, able diplomat never much troubled by self doubt, had been UK Ambassador in Brussels during those tricky New Zealand negotiations in the wake of the *Rainbow Warrior* affair, and before that our paths had crossed when he was a member of the British Mission in Brussels at the time of Britain's negotiation to join the EEC .

In the same way I had previous engagement with senior UN Secretariat officials from my time in Geneva, including Kofi Annan, who became peacekeeping chief in the Secretariat before going on to a higher calling as the UN Secretary-General. These connexions proved an advantage. Given this it was difficult to grasp how someone parachuted in and inducted into the Security Council, without the benefit of front-line Head of Mission experience across the full range of UN responsibilities (which had also to be discharged alongside Security Council preoccupations) could improve the New Zealand performance or contribution.

Extolling diplomatic fraternisation in this way risks confirming popular scepticism that diplomacy amounts to an elitist pastime carried out surreptitiously by a charmed circle of insiders. But personal acquaintanceship in external relations does help smooth pathways, particularly when explaining and defending policy differences face-to-face with representatives of a government that plainly disagrees with New Zealand policy. Diplomacy cannot spin straw into gold, but it remains a venerable tool for managing relations between countries, and has a proven elasticity which is capable of being stretched to cover many eventualities, and to defuse strife.

ca

When New Zealand took its place at the Security Council table on 1 January 1993, the five permanent members with powers of veto – the US, UK, France, China and Russia – had agreed amongst themselves to suspend use of that veto. It was a so-called 'gentlemen's agreement'. The Cold War had, after all, just ended. There was a palpable sense of relief and hope that the UN might at last come into its own as an authentic agent for global peace and development. Suspending the veto theoretically opened the way for authentic negotiation around the Council table about suitable responses to global security threats, allowing a greater role for smaller non-permanent members in such negotiation.

The overriding nature of post–Cold War conflict, which soon became very clear, involved enmity *inside* borders not *across* borders. Yet the United Nations had been conceived in 1945 as an institution to prevent conflict *between* states not *within* states, so in the immediate post–Cold War situation the Security Council confronted profoundly sensitive issues of sovereignty when debating how (or whether) to legitimise intervention in countries where instability or inhumanity could not be ignored by outsiders. The agenda of crises before the Council in 1993 was long – Bosnia, Iraq, Somalia, Palestine, Angola, Cambodia, Rwanda, Mozambique, Western Sahara, North Korea, Libya, Cyprus, and more. It soon became clear to newcomers that the pressure to take swift and resolute decisions in times of internal conflict was often based on incomplete or even misleading information. In many cases an overhasty Security Council reaction was as problematic as inaction or neglect.

The point here was that Council newcomers had to learn very quickly. Without the menace of the veto in the immediate post–Cold War years, working methods were less structured and mediated than they have since become. They involved prolonged informal bargaining in a crowded side room adjacent to the Council chamber – late nights and weekend conclaves were standard. The Council President needed to have constant informal one-on-one sessions with the other 14 Council members to probe their bottom line on issues that were before the Council. Some of the crises were of a kind or involved a country for which, at other 'normal' times, New Zealand would never have concerned itself, or perceived a need to develop a considered policy response, let alone an immediate reaction. Council membership demanded changes to New Zealand habits of improvisation in haste.

CR

The Presidency of the UN Security Council rotates monthly in alphabetical order. After just two months on the Council it was New Zealand's turn in March 1993 to assume that role. The rapidly deteriorating situation in the former Yugoslavia monopolised attention, with Serb, Croatian and Muslim communities involved in bitter internal conflict, including ethnic cleansing. The Council had agreed that a United Nations Protection Force should be despatched, although its exact mandate was imprecise; at the same time a peace initiative backed by European governments, implicating all three of the warring communities, had been launched in Geneva under the joint chairmanship of former US Secretary of State Cyrus Vance and former UK Foreign Secretary David Owen.

The resultant Vance–Owen peace plan envisaged reconstituting the former Federal Republic of Yugoslavia (FRY) into a collection of separate cantons in the Swiss style, based around different ethnicities. It was a fraught plan, but in March 1993, as New Zealand took up the UN Security Council presidency, the two chairmen brought it to New York for Council endorsement. The leaders of the three warring ethnic communities also assembled in New York: Radovan Karadžić for the Serbs, Mate Boban for the Croats and Alija Izetbegović, who was President of Bosnia, for the Muslims. Liaising with Vance and Owen to pilot their plan through the Security Council, maintaining close contact with the UN Secretary-General, and brokering with the three community leaders were the key preoccupations during the New

Zealand Council presidency. The brokerage produced minimal results; the Serb leader rejected the plan, the Bosnian leader accepted it and the Croat leader was ambivalent.

The flawed Vance–Owen plan remained the only game in town, even as Council members (New Zealand included) harboured reservations. The brand new Clinton administration, however, swiftly took action that effectively disowned the plan, and the Russians soon followed suit. Matters were not helped by public criticisms of US by the notably undiplomatic Owen.

The New Zealand presidency piloted two decisions about the former Yugoslavia through the Council during March 1993 – to set up an International Criminal Tribune for war crimes in the region and urge compliance with the no-fly zone over the region. The able New Zealand Deputy Ambassador John McKinnon was involved with assuring a diligent drafting process for these decisions. Meanwhile things on the ground in FRY only got worse.

Aside from Bosnia, the New Zealand presidency had responsibility for piloting a Council decision for despatch of a new UN peacekeeping mission to Somalia to replace a former American-led contingent earlier installed there. The Clinton administration in Washington swiftly committed to American participation, which on the face of it seemed to break new ground: for the first time ever, it appeared the US would join a UN blue-helmet-led peacekeeping operation, one which at its height involved over 20,000 personnel drawn from a range of countries (including a New Zealand logistics support unit).

The reality proved quite different. The US set up a unique and confidential chain of command, quite separate from the UN blue-helmet command (under a Turkish general), the consequences of which proved disastrous. It led to the so-called Black Hawk Down firefight in the capital, Mogadishu, where 18 helicopter-borne US special forces were killed in an attack about which the UN commander was not informed (although the UN force did assist the extraction of the American troops). The US promptly withdrew all its contingent from Somalia, and henceforth exhibited distinct reticence about peacekeeping. The Black Hawk Down incident occurred just after my own departure from New York. It was deeply ironic that the US Congress's subsequent postmortem on the debacle blamed the UN. Not for the first time, nor the last, the UN provided a convenient scapegoat for powerful member states' deficiencies.

The worsening situation in Bosnia, in particular Serb atrocities after the capture of the town of Srebrenica, prompted the UN Security Council in April 1993 to agree to despatch a six-person mission of Council representatives for first-hand appraisal. I was asked by the Council President (Jamsheed Marker of Pakistan) to join the mission – led by the Venezuelan UN Ambassador Diego Arria (a wealthy political appointee with domestic political ambitions, who revelled in publicity) with Russian, French, Hungarian, Pakistani and New Zealand participants. There were a half dozen journalists in tow (BBC, NYT, CBS, Reuters, AFP), but once on the ground that number ballooned to over 40 (including CNN).

It was a harrowing expedition crammed into just six days, entailing much helicopter travel. Sarajevo, the capital, was a pitiable sight, pounded by Serb artillery from surrounding hills, with shattered streets, gutted buildings, wrecked vehicles, and Serb snipers. The pretty Muslim village of Ahmići had been ethnically cleansed by Croats – the mosque blown up, whole families killed – I visited one house with the incinerated bodies of two adults and four children lying amidst a carpet of bullet casings. Serb artillery had pulverised Srebrenica (one shell every seven seconds), and the school playground was covered in children's blood. Water and medical supplies were cut off by occupying Serb troops and UN relief supplies (blankets, tents, etc.) impounded. It was a picture of utter desolation; and it was to be repeated with a second bout of outrageous ethnic cleansing by Serb forces in 1995.

All three ethnic communities (Serb, Croat and Muslim) were guilty of atrocities, but only the Serbs were capturing and holding territory. The Security Council mission learnt that the UN peacekeeping contingent lacked basic assets like aerial reconnaissance, and its mobility was hobbled by the unwillingness of individual contingents to act upon the Swedish force commander's orders, unless first cleared with their individual capitals. There were disagreements too amongst the senior UN commanders over interpretation of the force's rules of engagement, and its right therefore to take preventive or punitive action.

The mission's report back to the Council was half baked. This was hardly surprising given the inherent differences of viewpoint represented within the mission itself. The report recommended the declaration of a number of 'safe areas' that required withdrawal forthwith by Serb forces, and did not rule out use of military force to defend or enforce the safe areas should the Serbs fail to comply. It was a sign of the prevailing ambivalence at the Council that its decision, taken on the basis of the mission's report, actually omitted all specific reference to enforcement.

The big powers (Britain and France) with peacekeeping contingents in Bosnia were leery about enforcement of 'safe areas' by means of aerial bombardment, fearing retaliation against their ground troops. Those without forces on the ground – and particularly the US – could afford to be more pugnacious about enforcement. Alignments amongst the 15 Council members shifted. The Americans evinced more sympathy for the Muslim (Bosnian government) cause, whereas the British and Russians effectively subscribed to the Serbs. New Zealand's position was closer to that of the Muslim members on the Council – Pakistan, Morocco and Djibouti – and therefore the US, who supported Bosnia's government.

Serb aggression was relentless and at last produced a more muscular Council response in June 1993, just as my departure from the Council loomed. The decision promoted by France called for more troop contributions to the UN peacekeeping command, and the application of force in and around 'safe areas', including air power, with member states 'acting nationally or through regional organizations'. This decision paved the way for eventual aerial bombing by NATO, but the persistent major power ambivalence was such that the first air strikes against Serb forces were not actually launched until 1995 – two years later.

଼

As UN Security Council President I encountered the UN Secretary-General at close quarters. Boutros Boutros-Ghali was an enigmatic figure. He appeared quick and decisive, with an engaging smile, and very self confident to boot. His temper was on a short fuse, and as Council President I had exposure to it. He instituted Secretariat reform but proved very conservative when it came to senior female appointments. To New Zealand's disappointment moreover he broke up the special Secretariat unit devoted to the Law of the Sea.

Boutros did not appear to put great store by UN ambassadors, especially those from smaller member states, while he readily name-dropped world leaders as friends to anyone who listened. Unlike his predecessor, he largely shunned informal Security Council meetings. As President of the Council in March 1993 I was instructed by the members to urge attendance upon Boutros, and failing that for him to designate a respected personal representative – which he eventually did in the person of a former senior Indian diplomat.

From the outset of his term in 1992, Boutros had a good relationship with French President François Mitterand, but he did not enjoy unqualified American support, and he clashed with Washington openly over Bosnia. As an Egyptian his standing amongst UN Middle Eastern ambassadors was ambiguous. One leading Arab envoy described him privately as 'a stick of gelignite in a bottle of scent'. All things considered it was little surprise that Boutros only served one term as Secretary-General – the only incumbent, so far, ever to have done so.

The pace of work at the UN Security Council over the first six months of 1993 was intense. A total of 41 resolutions and decisions were adopted. To compare this with previous New Zealand experience, in 1953/54 when New Zealand served a two-year term the Council adopted a total of just seven such resolutions/decisions; and in 1966, during New Zealand's one-year tenure, 13 decisions/resolutions were endorsed. Those were the years when East–West Cold War paralysis by veto gripped the UN Security Council. The new intensity was most certainly not evidence that the post–Cold War Security Council was more effective or successful; it was due to the sheer complexity of post–Cold War challenges to security, which originated primarily in regional/internal conflicts. The work and the long hours required in the New Zealand Mission to manage New Zealand's involvement throughout the Security Council's highly complex decision-making process was confounding. Over the full two years of the New Zealand term, 1993–1994, the Security Council adopted a grand total of 171 resolutions and decisions.

As the date approached for my premature departure from New York in mid-1993, there had been no alternative employment on offer. I was effectively told at the outset that I would have to take 'pot luck'. Late in the piece, in the midst of fervent Security Council lobbying, I was urged by the Ministry hierarchy to allow my name to go forward for the position of Deputy Secretary-General of the Commonwealth Secretariat in London. That proposition was leaked too in Wellington to *Trans Tasman* although I had indicated I was not at all interested in the job. After persistent telephone persuasion, I reluctantly succumbed.

I had an amiable interview in New York with the Commonwealth Secretary-General Emeka Anyaoku, who soon afterwards informed me that another candidate had been selected. I was not in the least disappointed; I knew the British had fielded a candidate with the not unreasonable expectation, as the paymaster of the Commonwealth, that he would be chosen. So it proved. Interestingly, the tenure of the proposed Deputy position extended out to 1999, which was the same year that Don McKinnon had his hat in the ring for the Secretary-General position. Had I filled the Deputy role, New Zealand ambitions could have appeared excessive.

At the eleventh hour an offer of a senior Asian posting emerged, but by this time Elizabeth and I opted for going home. We were both fatigued by the prolonged uncertainty and the perverse expectations of us. There was one last twist to the tail. The news of my departure had now circulated in the UN corridors, and elicited surprise and reproach from several quarters, including from ambassadors who had cast valuable votes in New Zealand's favour and inferred they had been misled by the New Zealand decision to change its Security Council representative mid-stream.

On top of this, out of the blue the London satirical magazine *Private Eye* then carried a short piece to the effect that the New Zealand Ambassador to the UN was being bounced out following complaints to Wellington from the British Government. I contacted the New York journalist, who was a stringer for the magazine, to suggest he had hold of the wrong end of the stick, but in so doing I realised he might have access to information denied me. The *Private Eye* 'revelation' belongs entirely in the dustbin of history. But it set hares running amongst New Zealand media, who pursued me once I was back in Wellington. Inside the Ministry I encountered condolences and discomfort about my treatment from some colleagues.

10. ABSCONDING AT TWILIGHT

Back in Wellington, an opportunity presented itself for moving outside the MFAT box into more independent space. Foreign Minister Don McKinnon had, in the course of telephone exchanges as I readied to quit New York, mentioned an idea for establishing an independent Strategic Studies Centre attached to Victoria University of Wellington (VUW). He encouraged my interest, and I was glad that he did.

The invention of strategic studies as a subject worthy of serious attention dates from Britain around about the 1950s, notably with the establishment in London of the International Institute for Strategic Studies. It derived from a belief that it is entirely possible to form intelligent opinions about bigger picture issues affecting a country's interests, without having access to highly classified information. It was sustained too by the happy illusion that think tank ideas (or at least some of them) would be taken seriously in the corridors of power. It did not deny that academics should leave the bureaucrats to run the country's affairs, but it believed that the bureaucrats should listen to what academics, or outside specialists, had to say.

In the US too, strategic studies think tanks mushroomed in the second part of the last century. Several, notably those in Washington, operated 'revolving doors', in the sense that individuals from their ranks often moved into government positions, and vice versa, whenever there was a change of President. Different administrations favoured different think tanks whose output reflected or influenced prevailing official opinion: the Heritage Foundation was esteemed by the Reagan Administration, the Brookings Institution by Clinton and the Democrats, the Hoover Institution by the Trump Administration, and so forth.

The unexpected end of the Cold War in 1990, the opportunities and risks of globalised interdependence, the manifest influence upon New Zealand of successful newly industrialising countries in East Asia, and changes within New Zealand itself, not least in its patterns of migration, all strengthened the case for study and reflection about New Zealand's changing place in the world. The idea for an independent entity outside government to help this process seemed timely. Moreover the very concept of security (especially for smaller countries) extended increasingly beyond the military dimension to encompass the dangers posed by environmental threats and heedless resource exploitation, as well as the influences of technology and the distortions fuelling inequality in the world (including trade protectionism), and these all warranted a place in New Zealand's strategic reflection.

I was invited to draft the mission statement for an independent strategic studies centre, which I did after some due diligence. The Victoria University Vice Chancellor, Professor Les Holborow, was most supportive of the new venture, and Margaret Clark, Professor of Politics and International Relations, also welcomed me and the Centre on the campus. As start up for the new unit I was very fortunate that MFAT agreed to loan Adele Mason. We had worked together in Brussels and New York, and her common sense, efficiency and good cheer were indispensable. I secured too, at least on a part-time basis, Jim Rolfe as Deputy Director. He had a background in the Army and as a security policy adviser, and he later himself occupied the position of Director of the Centre.

A third colleague, Peter Cozens, also came on board. His interest was in maritime security and he was a particular advocate for a New Zealand oceans policy. He organised an early successful seminar on the subject, a first for New Zealand, but it proved ahead of its time – a quarter century later New Zealand still does not have such a policy. Peter also eventually became Director of the Centre and piloted it through some choppy water, mentioned below. We secured the services of Synonne Rajanayagam as a cool, calm, efficient secretary/organiser. We offered brief (unpaid) employment to David Capie as an intern, and secured employment too for Robert Ayson – both then young men destined for greater things in enhancing study and understanding about New Zealand's strategic future.

Beginning in 1993, the new Centre for Strategic Studies (CSS:NZ) at VUW had three connected goals: (1) to stimulate and expand connexions throughout the New Zealand academic community about strategic security thinking, comprehensively defined; (2) to encourage New Zealand media, at both the managerial and operational levels, towards greater utilisation of homegrown New Zealand opinion about international issues (there was marked preference for interpretative sound bites from Washington, London, Canberra, etc); (3) to project offshore the existence and interests of the new Centre and secure its membership of, and contribution to, the Council for Security Cooperation in Asia Pacific (CSCAP), which was the regional platform created in 1991/92 in Asia for study of strategic issues.

It was plain from the start that regional governments, especially those in the Association of Southeast Asian Nations (ASEAN), valued think-tank interchange – which they designated as 'Track Two', intended to complement the 'Track One' of official intergovernmental dealings. The collegiality, networking and personal contacts that were fostered on the Track Two circuit were considered to be an asset when deliberating about regional cooperation, grounded particularly in the ASEAN concept of 'security *with*' not 'security *against*' an identified (or implied) adversary. The United States' place as a resident of the Asian region was valued. At the same time a strategy dedicated manifestly to 'containing' China was disavowed. There was resistance to regional security alliance arrangements of the Atlantic variety, although some regional governments favoured individual bilateral security treaties with the US.

New Zealand had been much quicker out of the blocks in signing up to the Asia Pacific trade/economic Track Two channel – the Pacific Economic Cooperation Council, established in 1980 – this reflected the high priority New Zealand attached to trade. However, emerging strategic signals, particularly from an increasingly successful Southeast Asia, warned outsiders that concentration solely upon the prize of regional trade opportunity, in the absence of dedicated political trust building, would not cut the mustard. Cupboard love alone would be insufficient for New Zealand in Asia.

ASEAN preferences prevailed too in devising new architecture for Asia Pacific economic cooperation. Targets, rather than deadlines involving strict accountability, were set for trade and economic liberalisation.

The collective goal was defined as 'concerted unilateralism'. On the Victoria University campus the new Centre worked from the outset with Professor Gary Hawke, a principal New Zealand participant in the Asia Pacific Track Two economic process and Director of the Institute of Policy Studies, with which the Centre was twinned.

In order to become a member of CSCAP the Centre was required, under established rules, to establish a New Zealand National Committee. A cross section of participants were canvassed and agreed to serve under the Foreign Minister as Chair. Membership included a media owner, some editors, vice chancellors, a producer board head, economic researchers, a trade union leader, senior military and foreign affairs individuals and one ex-Governor-General. Such a cross-section hopefully illuminated the Centre's broad and independent base. Commentary, media interviews, publication of working papers and seminar reports, as well as extensive speaking engagements up and down the country, became commonplace and were intended to register the Centre's existence and raise its profile.

Externally a close relationship was established with the respected Malaysian Institute of Strategic and International Studies, with which the Centre hosted a series of seminars and working groups pinpointing the comprehensive and cooperative nature of joint security in the region. A pattern of wider connexions and activity then intensified to include China (in both Beijing and Shanghai), Vietnam (before establishment by New Zealand of a diplomatic presence), Japan, Indonesia, Thailand, the Philippines, Singapore, South Korea and North Korea. Visits and seminars in those various capitals ensued. Participation in Track Two seminars in the US, Canada and Australia were also part of the pattern. The Centre's budget included provision to fund participation by New Zealand academics in this regional activity, which helped broaden connexions for them individually and their universities, as well as for the Centre.

Connexions with North Korea broke entirely new ground. North Korean participants, for the first time anywhere, joined a 1995 working group hosted in Wellington and drawn from across the region which addressed the comprehensive nature of security for the region. The North Koreans then paid a second visit to New Zealand, which led to an invitation to the Centre for Strategic Studies for a nine-day return visit to North Korea in 1998. That was the first such invitation extended by the North Koreans to any Western strategic think tank.

We had discussions in Pyongyang and beyond with the Foreign Ministry, Trade Commission, clothing factory bosses, and port authorities, as well as a visit to Kaesong, with its cross-border Industrial Region jointly operated by North and South Korea, and the nearby Demilitarised Zone, where I inspected a guard of honour and lunched with the deputy commander, a colonel who spoke excellent English. From the latter vantage point we gazed southwards to the 'free world', in sight of hard-faced South Korean and US military guards. Throughout, the visit was carefully choreographed by the hosts. The fierce commitment to self reliance (juche), with its inspiration derived directly from the leadership of North Korea's founder Kim Il Sung, was constantly reiterated.

At one point I asked my host why the North Korean think tank had selected the New Zealand Centre for special attention. He replied to the effect that the North Koreans knew New Zealand had experienced difficulties with the Americans over issues related to nuclear weapons, and that they too had similar problems. There was a common concern. I then explained the essential differences in our respective situations, emphasising New Zealand's strong commitment to nuclear disarmament. The visit occurred before North Korea openly proclaimed and demonstrated nuclear weapon capability.

All in all the short visit was an experience beyond ready understanding, and present day North Korea has undoubtedly witnessed change, at least in terms of modernisation in its capital and the economic expectations of its urban population. The three-person CSS:NZ team finally departed by rail on the unsuitably named Pyongyang–Beijing Express, in which we lumbered for 24 hours to the Chinese capital in locked carriages, assailed by foul-smelling North Korean cigarette smoke. The journey was redeemed somewhat at the Chinese border by the attachment to the train of a dining and bar car, full of roistering Chinese businessmen returning to Beijing.

∝

The Centre's growing connexions across the region stimulated two-way traffic, which included secondment to the Centre of a Chinese scholar and of Japanese scholars, thanks to generous funding from the Asia

New Zealand Foundation. A large Chinese military delegation from the People's Liberation Army visited the Centre in 1998, where a veritable platoon of generals and other top-level brass explained to a well attended presentation the dimensions of China's first ever White Paper on Defence. The Chinese were in fact scheduled for a groundbreaking visit to Washington for precisely the same purpose, and the delegation had opted for a dress rehearsal in Wellington – that at least was the explanation volunteered by an accompanying Chinese diplomat.

Our interactions with Australian think tanks and universities brought home the impressive efforts the Australians were making to deepen strategic security perceptions and understanding of Asia. The new and well endowed Lowy Institute in Sydney was a prime example, but there were others. Although New Zealand could in no way emulate the Australians, there were object lessons aplenty.

One was the essential strategic difference behind our respective viewpoints. Australia's ambition for the status of 'middle level power' involved an arm-in-arm relationship with the US and its strategic designs, and this was reflected in much (but by no means all) of the output from Australia's Track Two strategic studies establishment – especially from think tanks closest to Canberra. Paul Dibb, the Director of the Strategic and Defence Studies Centre at the Australian National University and author of a definitive official study on Australian defence strategy (the Dibb Report), was then a leading disciple, with close affinity for US political/security interests and projects. Several dealings with him revealed an abiding scepticism about China and its intentions, together with a hearty dismissal of diplomacy as a means to create a peaceable region.

The ways in which the trans-Tasman partners, together or apart, continue to respond to China will surely condition their future relationship one with another. As the smaller party, and absent middle level power ambition, New Zealand perceptions will always likely differ in some particulars at least. After all, on its own account New Zealand has already spent nearly 50 years putting runs on the board with China. It will presumably resist therefore any notion that Australia (or indeed anyone else) gets to decide the acceptability of particular New Zealand relationships in East Asia. Adjustment to China by both countries will be influenced, to a greater or lesser extent, by (a) the relative weighting attached at any one time to an 'interests' driven or a 'values' driven foreign policy and (b) how China's neighbours – especially in Southeast Asia, who have lived for centuries in China's shadow, and provide the doorstep to Asia for the two Tasman countries – make a virtue of necessity in fashioning their relationships with Beijing.

⟶

Domestically it was a novel experience to look close up at official conduct of New Zealand's external interests. There was a risk, of course, that the two Ministries (Defence and Foreign Affairs) who along with Victoria University were supporting the Centre, might find toleration of the Centre's independence to be a test. On particulars – like an early study commissioned by the Centre in favour of New Zealand banning the use of land mines, whose utility was valued by the New Zealand Defence Force (NZDF) and by the Americans – the study was not, to NZDF's credit, suppressed. Officialdom tolerated too a muffled drumbeat from the Centre that New Zealand defence policy needed to balance its traditionally preferred US/Europe alignments, and cultivate an authentic Asian dimension involving joint operations (including peacekeeping) with Asian militaries. A further proposition, however, that the post–Cold War status of 'friend but not ally' of the US actually now suited New Zealand, both logically and substantively, seemed a bridge too far for formal acknowledgement by officials.

In the domain of foreign policy, the Centre argued the case for New Zealand's deployment in March 1994 to the UN peacekeeping operation in Bosnia, whilst MFAT and its Minister opposed that idea. In the case of the US-led attack upon Iraq in 2004, a total disaster, the Centre's contribution, which was discussed at a senior political level, included a recommendation that New Zealand stand apart from involvement, just as the government itself was coming to that decision. New Zealand policy advisers were still themselves weighing up the fact that Australia was opting to join the Americans.

In trade policy, CSS:NZ made efforts to nudge history. After an exchange with Sir Frank Holmes, New Zealand's leading academic economist, regarding New Zealand's consistent failure over many years to interest the US in a free trade agreement, he concurred with the idea that New Zealand should leave that bid on the table, but actively pursue other avenues, in particular with China. Op-ed pieces were produced out of the Centre in 2002 and 2003 commending such an approach. There was no evidence at the time that this registered at all with New Zealand trade policy advisers, for whom an American deal remained an absolute number one priority. The Chinese Ambassador to Wellington, however, a shrewd active diplomat, signalled in private conversation that he had read the advocacy and was thinking on the idea. Many competent hands subsequently combined to launch negotiations with China in 2004 and bring the New Zealand–China Free Trade Agreement to fruition in 2008 – a notable first for New Zealand and for China. But as they rightly say: 'Success has a thousand fathers, while failure is an orphan.'

— ∞ —

It had been a surprise to realise in the Centre that New Zealand policy makers, when pondering the country's strategic future, had felt no real requirement to factor in the end of the 40-year Cold War. The clear message conveyed by the 1991 Defence of New Zealand (DONZ) publication, the first New Zealand post–Cold War White Paper, was basically 'business as usual'. Significant changes in East Asia and their clear implications for New Zealand were viewed in the DONZ from the perspective of a need for New Zealand to be prepared to commit to preserve Western ideals, interests and advantages in the region. There was no sense that national interest might require New Zealand to adjust defence policy alongside other policies; to cultivate, in its own right, closer ties with a region where, plainly, New Zealand's economic future would be made. In all of this there was space for the new Centre of Strategic Studies to be intrepid.

Meanwhile, of course, New Zealand was participating with others in laying the foundations for political and economic architecture to underpin regional cooperation (Asia-Pacific Economic Cooperation – APEC). It was not doing this as a 'representative of Western interests', with first allegiance to the North Atlantic world or its models and policies. Asian governments clearly intended the architecture to be indigenous to the region and its needs, not imported from elsewhere. At the same time New Zealand was also fashioning itself a suite of new bilateral connexions with individual Asian and Pacific countries, not all of them democratic – in education, immigration, tourism, information technology, computer software, lifestyle, cinema and the like.

All this highlighted an enduring anomaly. Public and formal expressions of New Zealand attitudes to strategic change are in effect confined solely to periodic Defence White Papers. A more integrated, inclusive national security statement, taking account of multiple challenges affecting New Zealand's interests and its sense of place in the world, is lacking. The result is dissonance, witnessed especially where New Zealand Defence White Papers assert, in loyal step with equivalent Australian and American documents, that a key role for NZDF lies with traditional partners in protecting the rules-based international order.

There are obvious immediate problems here if or when those traditional partners are themselves serially ignoring international rules. President Donald Trump was not the first US leader to disregard international agreements. At the beginning of the present century George W. Bush's warlike administration disavowed restraints of international law in pursuing 'preventive war' (war now to prevent war later) and 'regime change' to overthrow uncongenial governments.

The extent to which President Trump baldly asserted the extra-territorial reach of America's law, and sanctioned rivals and partners alike to compel support for American objectives, exceeded what had gone before, but whether the Trump administration will be judged by history as a total aberration, or alternatively as something of a bellwether for future US behaviour, is not the point here. The point is that New Zealand judgements about care and observance of international law are not subjects solely or principally for defence and security policy. They are primarily a concern for New Zealand foreign policy.

An integrated national security statement was attempted, but never repeated, in June 2000 in the document 'New Zealand's Foreign and Security Policy Challenges' issued under the name of Foreign Minister Phil Goff. It was eclipsed subsequently by the thunderclap of the September 2001 (9/11) terrorist attacks on the US, a defining moment in modern history. A declaration by the US of a 'global war on terror' was instantly proclaimed, thus providing a new-made organising principle for American global leadership. In several places there were doubts about the wisdom of this declaration – terrorism is after all a tactic, not a country. One most respected British authority, the distinguished Professor of War History at Oxford University Sir Michael Howard, described the American policy as a 'hunter's licence to use force anywhere in the world, and the right to dispense with the restraints of international law'.

Reconfiguration of American national security policy after the shock of 9/11 produced even greater concentration of security and intelligence policymaking around the executive in the White House. Diplomacy was, to most intents and purposes, pigeonholed, and Washington encouraged friends and allies to reconfigure accordingly. Although not a formal American ally, New Zealand officials were clearly influenced by the 'Five Eyes' intelligence-sharing arrangement with the US, UK, Canada and Australia, and New Zealand political and security policymaking gravitated towards the Prime Minister's Office. As the only Five Eyes partner with no hard power, however, any pigeonholing of New Zealand's diplomacy would clearly be self defeating. It is not sufficient after all that New Zealand relies internationally upon the limiting strictures of 'balance of power' thinking, which traditionally influences security/intelligence specialists, but which narrows the foundations for well rounded appreciation of external change.

If New Zealand opts to remain in Five Eyes it should do so only on the basis that, at the bottom line, intelligence does not make foreign policy, it serves foreign policy; although in the case of the US, and of Australia, intelligence plainly carries the greater weight and has even (as witnessed in the 2004 attack on Iraq) been expediently concocted in ways to justify war. Five Eyes is not a formal alliance treaty; it is an expedient arrangement between intelligence agencies to exchange information. At times of intense rivalry between the great powers it should be no surprise that information shared by the US, given its robust rivalry with China, should reflect its compulsive priority. In those circumstances New Zealand should commit formally as well to widen exchanges of intelligence with Asia-Pacific partners.

As this present century began, New Zealand foreign policy conduct overall benefitted from greater resources allocated to MFAT under Foreign Minister Winston Peters. As part of this extending virtuosity, the case can be made for investment in a greater long-term analytical capability inside the Ministry that draws upon judgements and deductions derived from its overseas diplomatic network, so as to provide New Zealand-grounded political intelligence to set alongside material coming down the Five Eyes pipeline.

ଔ

Limits to official tolerance of the Centre for Strategic Studies' independence remained an occupational hazard. That was directly demonstrated in 1999 when the Centre organised a seminar to consider a report entitled 'Defence Beyond 2000' by Parliament's Foreign Affairs, Trade and Defence Committee under the chairmanship of Derek Quigley MP. The document was an unorthodox and entirely novel New Zealand approach to future defence planning, as it involved politicians and not government officials in a lead role. Invitations to the Centre's seminar went out to all the usual suspects, including Minister of Defence Max Bradford, as well as his officials. The Minister for some unaccountable reason remained oblivious to that fact, for he wrote me a short letter on the eve of the seminar, protesting his non-inclusion in terms that questioned the Centre's objectivity and credibility.

I was at the time seeking a two-year extension of my contract, due to terminate in 1999. The purpose was to explore further the idea of an actual teaching role for CSS:NZ (although I would not myself have been involved). The Centre had received a tick of approval in a recent audit of performance and I had reason to believe the teaching proposal was looked upon favourably. I was disappointed then to learn following an interview (that occurred on the same day as the seminar) that my proposed two-year extension was refused; the Deputy Director of the Centre, David Dickens, was instead appointed to the position.

The coincidence between the Minister of Defence's curt and recriminatory letter and this decision not to extend my term seemed more than just serendipity. The Parliamentary Committee under Derek Quigley launched an enquiry. This found there had been no involvement by the Minister of Defence in the appointment decision, but that the protest letter to me about the seminar (which was highly unusual practice) contributed to a perception that such involvement could have occurred. The Committee's investigation (published in August 1999) records testimony by a substantial list of witnesses, from the Minister of Foreign Affairs and the Secretary of Defence (but not the Minister, intriguingly), downwards. Reading it provided a sober lesson in self awareness.

As a postscript, the Centre struck choppy water under the new Director. His affiliation with the National Party (of which I had been unaware) provided a complication after the 1999 general election: National lost, and Dickens soon moved on. A replacement was sought in quick order – Peter Cozens was selected and he steadied the ship from 2002 to 2009. He introduced the designation of Senior Fellows for the Centre (a common feature in many overseas think tanks) and kindly invited me to become one. My association with the Centre endured.

∾

My experience at the Centre for Strategic Studies confirmed my sense that in a world of great power rivalry, there is consolation for New Zealand from insignificance: the country threatens no one, yet possesses authentic soft power and travels internationally beneath the radar screens of the powerful. Discrete geography at times of such high-pressure rivalry can be advantageous, provided that New Zealand cultivates an informed strategic mentality backed by agility and discernment. Fears about New Zealand being marginalised internationally, which so animated official advisers at times covered by this memoir, no longer constitute an inescapable fate when technologies of communication have collapsed space, distance and time. Marginalisation becomes an act of choice, not inevitable destiny, although relationship-building nonetheless necessitates acute judgement at times between New Zealand values and New Zealand interests.

Judgements about moral equivalence in foreign relations are tricky – it is difficult to know, for example, where precisely to draw the line between an imperious, authoritarian China with a dubious human rights reputation, and a powerful US that itself disregards international rules, is beset with deep internal strife and is convinced China's rise must be halted if US primacy and national security interests are to be preserved. A persistent shoving match for influence between the US and a re-emergent China will very likely remain a reality of international relations even as there is a distinct ingredient of 'pots calling kettles black' in the mutual exchanges of recrimination. New Zealand's potential to navigate and adjust to such disharmony will be tested, but the accumulated experience and adjustments forced upon it by external change over the past generation and a half of relationship building stand the country in good stead.

☾

There were diversions from the new Centre's key preoccupations with Asia. In 1997 it was asked to put together a New Zealand team to participate at a British Foreign Office seminar in Sussex on future NZ–UK relations. This was chiefly notable for the fact that the initiative for it had come from the British. They assembled businesses, politicians and academics with an interest in New Zealand, amongst them former UK Permanent Under-Secretary of State for Defence Sir Michael Quinlan. He was a person of formidable intellect and considered to be the leading apostle of nuclear deterrence and British nuclear weapon ownership.

His forthright contribution at the seminar robustly condemned New Zealand non-nuclear policy with its threat to 'the seamless web of Western security'. Sir Michael had actually visited New Zealand earlier in the year and I had been somewhat surprised then to be asked to debate with him 'What Future for Nuclear Weapons', moderated by the broadcaster Ian Fraser. It was a well attended occasion at Parliament and the result was polite and respectful agreement to disagree. The event in Sussex provided a second round on home turf, and witnessed a notable gloves-off contribution by Sir Michael.

Discussion at the seminar ranged far wider than just nuclear policy. The New Zealand team consisted of the historian James Belich; ex-Governor-General Sir Paul Reeves; Fran Wilde, CEO of Trade New Zealand, former Labour Party minister and former Mayor of Wellington; and John Falloon CNZM, former National Party minister. The New Zealand High Commissioner to London, Dick Grant, also contributed. On the eve of the encounter, the event was overshadowed by the death of Diana, Princess of Wales in a car accident in Paris.

☾

Lessons from modern international relations teach just how completely and swiftly unforeseen (or unforeseeable) events can capsize previous assumptions about external and domestic affairs. At the time of writing, the vehement shock of the 2020 COVID-19 pandemic has engulfed a largely unprepared world. Intrinsic features of global interdependence have been confounded – cross-border flows of people, goods, technologies, systems of outsourcing and supply chain trade simply and starkly blown off track.

Hindsight will eventually determine the full extent, scope and duration of the impacts. Unsurpassed levels of government intervention involving massive borrowing to offset, in particular, ballooning unemployment, together with diminished faith in market forces to supply remedies, signalled profound consequences everywhere. New Zealand's external relations future will be shaped by an international context that has now been invaded by COVID-19 and its aftermath.

The deepening dimensions of global interdependence, between issues and between countries, are starkly illuminated by COVID-19. They compel greater cooperative vigilance between governments. The present age is one where brave new technologies have massively amplified capacity for gathering information and intelligence, allowing governments (at least theoretically) to anticipate change, to predict danger and to facilitate timely responses. The actual record, however, falls way short. Great power rivalry includes fierce competition to develop and safeguard the intellectual property of those brave new technologies, as part of a zero-sum game of winners and losers stretching from cyber software and hardware to medicine and new vaccines.

Rationally, the universal COVID-19 threat should have commanded an instant international communal response. Yet the first reactions by many countries were downright nationalistic. There were different explanations, but it was impossible to deny that the machinery of international cooperation generally had been corroded by the go-it-alone behaviour of principal powers well before the pandemic. The world has no interest in pandemic recovery being hindered and divided by great-power rivalry; the same applies, with bells on, in respect to the supreme global challenge of climate change.

The response to COVID-19 cannot reinforce confidence that international cooperation will be readily secured unless a fundamental change of heart occurs in the emerging rivalry between the US and China. This the space wherein New Zealand needs to retain evenhandedness and the essential logic of a distinctive small-power contribution of the kind displayed through its non-nuclear policy, which remains an eminently rational and respectable hallmark of New Zealand's approach towards foreign affairs.

ACRONYMS

Asia Pacific Economic Cooperation	APEC
Association of Southeast Asian Nations	ASEAN
Australia–New Zealand Closer Economic Relations Trade Agreement	ANCERTA; CER
Australia, New Zealand and United States Security Treaty	ANZUS Treaty
Centre for Strategic Studies	CSS:NZ
Common Agricultural Policy	CAP
Commonwealth Heads of Government Meeting	CHOGM; HOG
Convention on the Regulation of Antarctic Mineral Resource Activities	CRAMRA
Council for Security Cooperation in Asia Pacific	CSCAP
Department of External Affairs	DEA
Department of Scientific and Industrial Research	DSIR
Directorate-General for External Security (France)	DGSE
Economic Commission for Asia and the Far East	ECAFE
Economic Commission for Asia and the Pacific	ESCAP
European Commission	EC
European Economic Community	EEC
Exclusive Economic Zone	EEZ
External Assessments Bureau	EAB
Federal Republic of Yugoslavia	FRY
Foreign & Commonwealth Office	FCO
Front de Libération Nationale Kanak et Socialiste	FLNKS

General Agreement on Tariffs and Trade	GATT
International Labour Organisation	ILO
International Monetary Fund	IMF
International Whaling Commission	IWC
Law of the Sea	LOS
Melanesian Spearhead Group	MSG
Ministry of External Relations and Trade	MERT
Ministry of Foreign Affairs	MFA
Ministry of Foreign Affairs and Trade	MFAT
New Zealand–Australia Free Trade Agreement	NAFTA
New Zealand Defence Force	NZDF
New Zealand Press Association	NZPA
Non-Governmental Organisations	NGOs
North Atlantic Treaty Organization	NATO
Organisation of African Unity	OAU
Organization for Economic Co-operation and Development	OECD
Overseas Development Assistance	ODA
Overseas Handbook	OSH
Overseas Marketing Board	OMB
Royal New Zealand Air Force	RNZAF
Royal New Zealand Navy	RNZN
Southeast Asia Treaty Organisation	SEATO
South Pacific Applied Geoscience Commission	SOPAC
South Pacific Regional Trade and Economic Cooperation Agreement	SPARTECA
Soviet Union (Union of Soviet Socialist Republics)	USSR
Total Allowable Catch	TAC
United Nations Committee on Disarmament	UNCD
United Nations Conference on Trade and Development	UNCTAD
United Nations Human Rights Committee	HRC

United Nations Security Council	UNSC
Victoria University of Wellington	VUW
World Health Organization	WHO
World Intellectual Property Organization	WIPO
World Meteorological Organization	WMO
World Trade Organization	WTO

TERENCE O'BRIEN

6 January 1936 – 30 December 2022

Year	Posting/Position	Location
1936	Born in Aylesbury, Buckinghamshire, United Kingdom	Aylesbury
1959	Joins the New Zealand Department of External Affairs	Wellington
1962	Becomes a naturalised New Zealand citizen	Wellington
1963	Second Secretary, New Zealand Embassy to Thailand	Bangkok
1966	Second Secretary, New Zealand Embassy to the United Kingdom	Wellington
1968	First Secretary, New Zealand Embassy to the European Union in Brussels	Brussels
1972	Deputy-Director, Housing Division, Ministry of External Relations and Trade	Wellington
1975	New Zealand High Commissioner to the Cook Islands	Rarotonga
1977	Deputy-Director, New Zealand Aid Division, Ministry of External Relations and Trade	Wellington
1980	New Zealand Ambassador to the United Nations in Geneva	Geneva
1983	New Zealand Ambassador to the European Economic Community and Denmark	Brussels
1986	Director, Pacific Division, Ministry of External Relations and Trade	Wellington
1990	New Zealand Ambassador to the United Nations in New York	New York
1993	Founding Director of the New Zealand Centre for Strategic Studies	Wellington
1999	Retires from the New Zealand Ministry of Foreign Affairs and Trade after 40 years of service	Wellington
2000	Serves as a Senior Fellow to the New Zealand Centre for Strategic Studies	Wellington
2016	Terence O'Brien scholarship established	Wellington
2022	Died in Wellington, New Zealand	Wellington

INDEX

Numbers in italics refer to pages in the
photograph section

A View from the Top, 141
Absolum, Brian, 71
AFP (Agence France-Presse), 151
Africa, 109, 132, 140, 143
Against the Odds, 55
Ahmići, 151
Air France, 33
Air Nauru, 71
Air New Zealand, 67–68, 74, 80, 82, 117
Akarana, *9*, 125
Albright, Professor Madeleine, 129–130
Andriessen, Frans, 108
Angola, 148
Annan, Kofi, 147
Ansell, Graham, 122, 130
Ansett Airways, 71
Antarctica, 82, 127
Anthony, Doug, 87
Antwerp, 60
Anyaoku, Emeka, 154
ANZAC Day ceremonies, 109–110
Apia, 118
Ardennes forest, 60
Arnett, Peter, 34
Arria, Diega, 151
Asia New Zealand Foundation, 159–160
Asia-Pacific Economic Cooperation
(APEC), 144, 162–163
Association of Southeast Asian Nations
(ASEAN), 157–158
Atiu, 68

Auckland, 104–105, 125
Auckland Hospital, 69
Australia, 36, 57, 69, 85, 110, 164
PNG aid, 43
South Pacific relations, 112–113, 115–
116, 118–122
trans-Tasman relations, 18, 81, 100,
122–127, 160–161
Australian National Maritime Museum,
126
Australian National University, 160
Australia–New Zealand–United States
(ANZUS) military alliance, 18, 112,
122–123, 125, 128
Avatiu Harbour, 75
Aylesbury, 11
Ayson, Robert, *16*, 156

Baghdad, 146
Bangkok, 12, 17–18, 21, 22–30, 32–35,
44
Bangkok Sports Club, 26
Banque National de Paris building, 105
Barnier, Michel, 54
Barre, Raymond, 91
Bavadra, Timoci, 116–117
Bay of Islands, 122–123
BBC, 56, 151
Beattie, Sir David, 117
Beaumont College (UK), 11
Beazley, Kim, 124–125
Beeby, Chris, 89, 106, 127
Beijing, 35–39, 158–159, 161
Beijing Airport, 37–38

Belgium, 50, 60, 95
Belich, James, 167
Bellamys, 19
Bennett, Peter, 120
Bergman, Ingmar, 89
Bikini Atoll, 114
Binh Dinh, 29
Blackpool, 48
Blakeley, Roger, 137
Blundell, Sir Denis, 72–73
Blunt, Sir Anthony, 72
Board of Trade (UK), 46–47
Boban, Mate, 149–150
Bolger, Jim, *10, 11, 12, 13*, 131, 134, 137, 140–142, 146
Bolger, Joan, 141
Bonn, 101
Bosnia, 144, 146, 148–153, 161
Bougainville, 115, 144
Boutros-Ghali, Boutros, *11*, 152–153
Bradford, Max, 165
Branch Davidian sect, 131
Brazil, 132, 137–138
Bremner, Brian, 39
Britain, 11, 36, 72, 80, 128, 131, 144, 154, 155, 164, 167
    EEC membership, 17, 93–94, 97–98, 108
    UN Security Council, 140, 146–148, 152
British Airways, 80
British Ambassador (Brussels), 58–59
British Embassy (Saigon), 33
British Foreign Office, 57–59, 101, 167
British High Commission, 20, 40
Brookings Institution, 82, 130, 155
Browne, Tony, 119
Bruges, 60
Brussels, 58–60, 81, 85, 147
    postings to, 12, 17–18, 46, 49–54, 91–92, 93–111, 145, 156
Brych, Milan, 69, 71, 73–75
Burke, Flying Officer, 109
Bush, Barbara, 141
Bush, George H.W., *12*, 137, 140–141
Bush, George W., 163

Byron, Lord, 84, 86

Cabinet Economic Committee, 44, 81
Cambodia, 28, 148
Canada, 36, 86–89, 137, 158, 164
Canberra, 116, 122, 126, 160
Capie, David, 156
Carrington, Lord, 101
Carter, Jimmy, 80
Castro, Fidel, 137
Caygill, David, 135
CBS, 151
Central Intelligence Agency (CIA), 108, 129
Centre for Strategic Studies, 12, 155–161
Chappaquiddick, 70
Charoen (cook), 23
Château de Chillon, 86
Chelsea, 46
Cheval Noir (Ypres), 110
China, 17, 35–39, 42, 66, 89, 121, 144, 146, 148, 157–162, 164, 166, 168
Chinese Embassy (Wellington), *3*, 38
Christchurch, 11, 22
Clark, Helen, 13
Clark, Professor Margaret, 156
Clausen, Tom, 91
Clinton, Bill, 129, 131, 144, 150, 155
Closer Economic Relations (CER), 81, 112, 126
CNN, 34, 151
Cold War, 49, 131, 148, 153, 156, 162
Columbus, Christopher, 131
Committee for Agriculture, 87
Common Agricultural Policy (CAP), 51–52, 94
Commonwealth Heads of Government (HOG), 118, 140–141, 144
Commonwealth Prime Ministers Conference, 74
Commonwealth Secretariat, 116, 127, 144, 154
Conservative Party (UK), 48
Cook Islands, 43, 62–76, 113
Coombs, Jane, *13*, 140
Cooper, Warren, 86, 95–96, 98

Copenhagen, 103, 108
Cotton, Paul, 48–49
Council for Security Cooperation in Asia
    Pacific (CSCAP), 157–158
Court of Appeal, 69
COVID-19 pandemic, 167–168
Cozens, Peter, 156, 166
Crete, 79
Cyprus, 148
Czechoslovakia, 69

Da Lat, 31
Dalmuir House, 40
Dalsager, Poul, 96, 98
Davies, Sonja, 124
Davis, Dr Tom, 70–71
Davis, Morrie, 80
Davos Economic Forum, 90
de Cuéllar, Javier Pérez, *10*, 106–107
de Gaulle, Charles, 47–48, 51
*Decision at Dawn: New Zealand and the
    EEC*, 55
Delors, Jacques, 106
Democratic Party (Cook Islands), 70–71
Deniau, Jean-Francois, 54
Denmark, 52–53, 93–95, 97, 103
Department of External Affairs, *1*, 12,
    15–16, 18–20, 24, 31, 33–35, 40,
    43–44, 61, 62, 65
Department of Island Territories, 43, 62,
    64
Department of Scientific and Industrial
    Research (DSIR), 68
Department of Trade and Industry, 17,
    81
DGSE, 104–105
Diana, Princess of Wales, 167
Dibb, Paul, 160
Dickens, David, 165–166
Djibouti, 152
Domestic and External Security
    Committee, 119–120
Donne, Gaven, 63, 71–73
Dortmund, 109
Douglas, Roger, 123
Duke of Marlborough, 60

Dumas, Roland, 106
Dunkel, Arthur, 86
Dunne, Peter, 135

East, Paul, 104
East Asia, 25, 156, 160, 162
East Timor, 144
Easterbrook-Smith, Geoff, *2, 5*
Economic and Social Commission for
    Asia and the Pacific (ESCAP), 24
Economic Commission for Asia and the
    Far East (ECAFE), 24–25
Edmonds, Paul, 34
Egypt, 153
Ellemann-Jensen, Uffe, 103
England, Natalie, 32–33
European Commission, 51–58, 93–102,
    105–107, 109–110
European Economic Community (EEC),
    17, 45, 47–58, 60, 81, 87–88, 93–94,
    96, 106, 108, 147
European Farm Council, 97–98, 108
European Parliament, 56, 104
European Union. *see* European
    Economic Community (EEC)
Evans, Gareth, 125
Exclusive Economic Zone (EEZ), 77–79
External Aid Division (MFA), 42–43
External Assessments Bureau (EAB), 20,
    129

Falloon, John, 167
Farnborough Airshow, 48
Fay, Sir Michael, 125
Federated Farmers, 137
Fergusson, Roy, 125
Fiji, 114–121
Fiji/New Zealand Businessmen's
    Council, 119
Financial Times, 107
Flanders, 60, 109
Flosse, Gaston, 122
Foreign Affairs, Trade and Defence
    Committee, 165–166
Foreign and Commonwealth Office
    (FCO), 45–47

France, 45, 47, 51, 54, 60, 91, 96–97, 99, 121, 127
  Rainbow Warrior, 104–108, 115–116
  UN Security Council, 146–148, 151–153
Francis, Tim, 129
Frankenstein, 84
Fraser, Ian, 167
Fraser, Malcolm, 81, 127
Freedom to Choose, 84
French Polynesia, 115, 122
Friedman, Milton and Rose, 84
Front de Libération Nationale Kanak et Socialiste (FLNKS), 115

Gallagher, Ken, 45
Galvin, Bernie, 43, 44–45, 48, 62
Gamble, David, 126
Ganilau, Penaia, 117
Gates, Rod, 116–117
General Agreement on Tariffs and Trade (GATT), 81, 83–88, 105
Geneva, 12, 17–18, 60, 81, 83-91, 96, 105, 133, 135, 137, 139, 145, 147, 149
Geneva International School, 84
Georgetown University, 129–130
Germany, 60, 91, 131
Ghana, 139
Ghent, 60
Glenarthur, Lord, 128
Gleneagles, 74
Goff, Phil, 163
Göring, Hermann, 56
Government House, 19
Grand Cravat Hotel (Luxembourg), 56–57
Grant, Dick, 77, 167
Gravensteyn, Achille, 105
Greece, 79
Greenpeace, 104
Greggs (Dunedin), 68
Guangzhou, 39
Gulf War, 146

Han Sung-joo, *13*
Hannay, David, 108, 140, 147

Harare, 140–141
Harland, Bryce, *2*, 36, 39–40
Hawke, Bob, *9*, 100, 113, 116, 118, 120, 124, 126–127
Hawke, Hazel, *9*
Hawke, Professor Gary, 158
Hayden, Bill, 100, 120, 122–123
Health Department, 69
Heath, Edward, 51
Helms, Jesse, 84
Henderson, John, 119, 123, 129
Henry, Sir Albert, *4*, 63–65, 67–76
Henry, Tupui, *3*, 75
Henry family (Cook Islands), 64
Hensley, Gerald, 119, 123
Hercus, Anne, 130
Heritage Foundation, 129, 155
High Commission for Refugees, 83
Hillary, Sir Edmund, 42
HMNZS *Wellington*, 117
Ho Chin Minh City, 29
Hodgkins, Frances, 58–59
Holborow, Professor Les, 156
Holmes, Sir Frank, 161–162
Holyoake, Sir Keith, 26–28, 31, 131
Hong Kong, 37–39
Hoover Institution, 155
Hotel Amigo (Brussels), 106–107
Hotel Caravelle (Saigon), 32–34
Howard, Sir Michael, 164
Hungary, 151
Hussein, Saddam, 147

India, 153
Indonesia, 26, 35, 42, 139, 158
Institute of Policy Studies, 158
International Dairy Arrangement, 96
International Dairy Products Council, 87–88
International Institute for Strategic Studies, 155
International Labour Organization (ILO), 83, 85
International Monetary Fund (IMF), 85, 90
International Red Cross, 83

International Whaling Commission (IWC), 48–49
Iran, 25
Iraq, 131, 146–148, 161, 164
Ireland, 52–53, 93, 97–98, 107
Irish Republican Army, 105
Ishkov, Aleksandr, 79
Italy, 109
Izetbegović, Alija, 149–150
Izvestia, 103

Japan, 58, 77–80, 88, 158–159
Jensen, Georg, 108
Jermyn, Ray, 67
Julin, M., 56–57

Kaesong, 159
Karadžić, Radovan, 149–150
Karika, Dame Margaret Makea Ariki, 76
Keating, Colin, 133
Keith, Kenneth, 144
Kelburn, 44
Kember, James, 140
Kennedy, John F., 34
Kennedy, Peter, 13
Kennedy, Teddy, 70
Kenny, Finbar, 69–71
Kerr, Roger, 50
Khon Kaen, 24
Khorat, 26, 30
Kim Il Sung, 159
King, Rodney, 131
King Baudouin (Belgium), 6
Kirchberg, 56–57, 98
Kiribati, 127–128
Kirk, Norman, 35, 69
Kirk government, 40–41, 43, 62
Kuwait, 131

Lange, David, 7, 9, 99, 103–104, 106–108, 113–114, 116–120, 122–123, 126, 128
Lange, Naomi, 9
Lange government, 99–100, 102–103, 113, 118, 124

Laos, 28, 42
Lapwood, Harry, 79
Latin America, 142–143
Law of the Sea (LOS), 77–78, 152
Libya, 119–120, 148
Lini, Walter, 114, 119–120
London, 12, 17, 20, 44–50, 53, 99, 101, 116, 155
Los Angeles, 131
Lower Hutt, 20
Lowy Institute, 160
Luxembourg, 50, 55–56, 60, 95, 98–100
Luxembourg Protocol, 96

Macdonald, Tom, 46
MacEachen, Allan, 86–87
Maclaurin, Cam, 32
Major, Sir John, 144
Malaysia, 26, 35
Malaysian Institute of Strategic and International Studies, 158
Malta, 132
Mandarin Hotel (Hong Kong), 39
Mangaia, 68
Mansfield, Michael, 35
Mansholt, Sicco, 51
Mao Zedong, 38–39
Māori Congress, 135, 138
Mara, Ratu Sir Kamisese, 116–119
Marker, Jamsheed, 151
Marshall, Russell, 7, 118–120, 124, 128
Marshall, Sir John, 24–25, 44, 54–57
Marshall Islands, 114
Mason, Adele, 140, 156
Matignon Accords, 115
Ma'uke, 68
McDowell, David, 35
McGibbon, Ian, 33
McGuire, Michael, 130
McIntosh, Alister, 18, 27, 34
McKinnon, Don, 134, 139, 143–145, 154, 155
McKinnon, John, 11, 150
McLean, Denis, 142
McLean, Fergus, 50

McPhail, Don, 86
Melanesian Spearhead Group (MSG), 121
Melbourne, 78
Memoirs, 54–55
Menzies, Sir Robert, 78–79
Messines, 109–110
Meyers, Marilyn, 129
Micronesia, 114
Milan Brych: The Cancer Man, 71
Miller, Rod, 38
Minister of Agriculture (Cook Islands), 67
Ministry for the Environment, 137
Ministry of Agriculture (UK), 47
Ministry of Defence, 129, 161
Ministry of External Relations and Trade (MERT), 16, 112, 117, 123–128, 130, 136, 139, 142
Ministry of Foreign Affairs and Trade (MFAT), 15–18, 41, 65, 89, 155–156, 161, 164–165
Ministry of Foreign Affairs (MFA), 16, 35–36, 40–43, 61, 77–82, 99, 106
Ministry of Transport, 68
Ministry of Transport and Civil Aviation, 80
Ministry of Works, 62
Mitiaro, 68
Mitterand, Francois, 137, 153
Moen, Commodore Karl, 119
Mogadishu, 150
Mondorf-les-Bains, 56
Mont Pelerin Society, 50
Montagnard tribes, 31
Montreal Olympic Games, 132
Moore, Mike, 5, 100, 102, 119, 124–126, 131, 133, 143
Moriarty, Jim, 47
Morocco, 152
Moscow, 20
Mount Erebus, 82
Mount Maunganui, 11
Moyle, Colin, 102–103
Mozambique, 148
Muldoon, Dame Thea, 74

Muldoon, Sir Robert, 4, 44–45, 68, 74–76, 78, 81, 90–91, 97–98
Muldoon government, 99, 112
Murdoch, Simon, 77, 126

Nadi Airport, 117
NASA, 70
Nash, Walter, 20
National Gallery (London), 59
National Party, 90, 131, 134, 166
National Security Council (US), 129
Nepal, 42
Netherlands, 60, 88
New Caledonia, 115–116
New York, 12, 18, 70, 106, 108, 129–130, 156
    posting to, 131–155
New York Times, 39–40, 151
New Zealand Aid Programme, 129
New Zealand Apple and Pear Marketing Board, 109
New Zealand Business Roundtable, 50
New Zealand Committee for the Australian Bicentenary, 125
New Zealand Dairy Board, 96
New Zealand Defence Force, 68, 161, 163
New Zealand Defence White Paper, 112, 122–123, 162–163
New Zealand Division, 26, 79
New Zealand Embassies
    Bangkok, 22–30, 32–34
    Beijing, 35–37
    Bonn, 90
    Brussels, 50–54, 105, 109
    Geneva, 83–91, 94
    Hong Kong, 25
    Jakarta, 25
    Kuala Lumpur, 25
    Paris, 32
    Saigon, 34
    Singapore, 25
    Tokyo, 25, 78
    Washington, 128–129
New Zealand High Commission (London), 20, 44–50

New Zealand House (London), 46
New Zealand Mission
  Brussels, 50–57, 93-111
  Geneva, 83-91
  New York, 132–154
New Zealand Press Association (NZPA), 27, 39, 47
New Zealand-Australia Free Trade Agreement (NAFTA), 81
New Zealand's Vietnam War, 33
Ngatipa (New Zealand Residence), 62–63, 65–66, 73
Ngo Dinh Diem, 31, 34
Nicolaidi, Mike, 27–28
Nikkhou-O'Brien, Maty, *16*
Niue, 65
Non-Aligned Movement, 139
Nong Khai, 28
non-nuclear policy, 18, 100–104, 107–108, 112–114, 122, 127, 129–130, 133–134, 141–144, 159, 167, 169
Norrish, Merv, 50, 58–59, 73, 112, 130
North Atlantic Treaty Organisation (NATO), 18, 100–101, 103, 152
North Korea, *16*, 148, 158-159
Nouméa, 115

O'Brien, Bridget, *1*, 11
O'Brien, Daniel, *14*, 12, 63, 145–146
O'Brien, Elizabeth (née Elworthy), *3*, *6*, *14*, *15*, 12, 22–23, 44, 46, 50, 59, 68, 74, 76, 84, 91–92, 109–110, 130, 146, 154
O'Brien, Georgia, *14*, 12, 59
O'Brien, Jane, 11
O'Brien, John, *14*, 12, 59
O'Brien, Peggy, *1*, 11
O'Brien, Timothy, *14*, 12, 76, 145–146
O'Brien, Wing Commander Oliver James (Paddy), *1*, 11–12, 20
O'Flynn, Frank, 102–103, 123–124
Ohakea, 120
O'Neill, Sir Con, 56
Operation Vietnam, 32
Organisation for Economic Cooperation and Development (OECD), 24, 41

Organisation of African Unity (OAU), 140
Otago University, 70
Overpelt, 109
Overseas Marketing Board, 102
Owen, David, 149–150
Oxford University, 12, 20, 164

Paal, Doug, 141
Pacific Economic Cooperation Council, 157
Pakistan, 151–152
Palais des Nations, 89
Palau, 114
Palestine, 148
Palmer, Sir Geoffrey, *9*, 101, 106, 113–115, 118, 127, 129, 131, 135
Papua New Guinea, 42–43, 115, 121
Paris, 41, 104, 167
Parliament Buildings, 18–19, 40, 78
Parliamentary Select Committee on Foreign Affairs, 124
Passchendaele, 109
Patrick, Charles, 87
Payton, David, 136
Pei Jianzhang, *3*
Penrhyn, 68
Pentagon, 129
People's Liberation Army, 160
Perry, Ray, 44–45
Peters, Winston, 16, 164
Philippines, 26, 35, 42, 158
Ploegsteert, 109
Pompidou, Georges, 51, 54
Pope, Arthur, 33
Prime Minister's Department, 44, 90
Princess Margaret, 89
Private Eye, 154
Pyongyang, 159

Qian Qichen, *13*
Queen Elizabeth II, 63, 71, 117
Queen Fabiola (Belgium), *6*
Queensland, 120
Queenstown, 95
Quigley, Derek, 165

Quill, Frank, 71
Quinlan, Sir Michael, 167
Quy Nhon, 29, 31–32

Rabuka, Colonel Sitiveni, 115–117, 119
Radio New Zealand, 113, 120
RAF 75 Squadron, 109–110
Rainbow Warrior, 104–108, 115–116, 147
Rajanayagam, Synonne, 156
Rarotonga, *3*, *4*, 17, 62–76, 83
Rarotonga Hospital, 69
Rarotonga Hotel, 74
Raumati Beach, *15*
Reagan, Ronald, 84, 129
Reagan Administration, 89, 155
Reesby Interiors, 38
Reeves, Sir Paul, 113, 117, 167
Reform, 106
Reuters, 34, 47, 151
Rex, Robert, *7*
Rio Environment Summit, 132–133, 135–139
Rippon, Geoffrey, 56–57
Robson, Mike, 55
Rocard, Michel, 115
Rolfe, Jim, 156
Rotorua, 79
Round, Derek, 39
Royal Hussars, 128
Royal New Zealand Air Force (RNZAF), 11, 26, 30, 37–38, 109, 114, 117, 120, 128
Royal New Zealand Navy (RNZN), 119, 124
Royal Society for the Prevention of Cruelty to Animals, 114
Russia, 88, 146, 148, 150–152
Rwanda, 148

Saigon, 29–34
Saint Joseph's Cathedral (Nouméa), 115
Salii, Lazarus, *7*
Samoa, 65, 118
Sarajevo, 151
Schmidt, Helmut, 91

Scotland, 74
Scowcroft, Brent, 141
Senegal, 139–140
Shackleton, Annabelle, 32
Shackleton, Michael, 32
Shanahan, Foss, *2*, 24–25
Shanghai, 158
Shelley, Mary, 84
Sheraton Hotel (Brussels), 95–96
Shields, Margaret, 104
Shultz, George, 112
Sinclair, Jonathan, *16*
Singapore, 158
Small, Tony, 134
Smith, Nick, 135
Smythe, Brian, 98
Solomon, Richard, 129
Solomon Islands, 121, 144
Somalia, 148, 150
Somaliland, 140
Sopé, Barak, 119–120
South Africa, 74, 132
South Korea, 77, 158–159
South Pacific, 17–18, 35, 41, 43, 65, 112–123, 127–129, 141, 143
South Pacific Forum, *7*, 17–18, 63, 114–115, 118, 121, 123, 127–128
South Pacific Policy Review Group, 113, 119, 123
Southeast Asia, 26, 28, 34–35, 157, 161
Southeast Asia Treaty Organisation (SEATO), 25–26
Soviet Embassy
  Bangkok, 25
  London, 49
Soviet Union, 49, 72, 77, 79, 103, 120, 131
Spain, 134, 143
Special Conference on Asian Economic Cooperation (ECAFE), *2*
Srebrenica, 151
SS Napier Star, 11
SS Perseus, 11
State Advances Corporation, 44
State Services Commission, 40
Stewart, Ian, 77–79

Storey, Rob, 137–138
Strasbourg, 104
Strong, Maurice, 137
Sussex, 167
Suva, 116–117, 119
Sweden, 134, 143, 151
Swiss government, 86
Sydney, 125–126, 160

Tahiti, 64
Talboys, Brian, *3*, 64, 73, 81, 95
Tan Son Nhut Air Base, 30
Tarawa, 127–128
TASS, 103
Tate Gallery, 59
Te Atairangikaahu, Te Arikinui Dame, 135, 138
Te Herenga Waka – Victoria University of Wellington, 12, 15, 155–158, 161
Teheran, 25
Templeton, Hugh, 81
Templeton, Malcolm, 77
Texas, 131
Thailand, 22–30, 35, 42, 158
Thatcher, Margaret, 93, 131
The Hague, 101, 144
Thompson, Gerry, 108
Thorn, Gaston, *5*, 99
Thulin, Ingrid, 89
Tivoli Gardens, 108
Tjibaou, Jean-Marie, 115
Tokelau, 65
Tokyo, 80
Tokyo Round, 87
Tolstoy, Leo, 27
Tonga, 114, 118, 122
Totokoitu Research Station, 68
Tourism Department, 74
Townsend, Group Captain Peter, 89
Trans Tasman, 145, 154
Treasury, 36, 43–44, 63, 90, 113, 123, 126
Tricot Report, 104
Trump, Donald, 163
Trump Administration, 155
Tupapa (Cook Islands), 66

Turkey, 134, 150
Turnbull Library, 124
Turner, Nick, 34
TVNZ, 28–29

United Nations, *10*, *11*, 24, 28, 70, 83–84, 106–108, 127, 130
    Building, *13*, 132
    Committee on Disarmament (UNCD), 83
    Conference on Trade and Development (UNCTAD), 83, 85
    General Assembly, 106, 132, 139–143, 146
    Human Rights Committee, 83
    peacekeepers, 150–152, 161
    Security Council, *10*, *11*, 18, 108, 129, 132–135, 138–139, 142–154
United States, 18, 25–26, 49, 55, 57–58, 68, 70–71, 80–82, 120, 131, 157–161, 166, 168
    9/11 terrorist attacks, 41, 163–164
    international trade views, 84–85, 88–89
    NZ relations, 100–101, 103, 106–108, 112–114, 122–123, 127–129, 133–134, 141–142, 144, 161–164
    Somalia conflict, 150–151
    strategic studies, 155
    UN Security Council, 146–148, 152–153
    Vietnam involvement, 29–35
United States Embassy (Saigon), 33
University College, Oxford, 12
University of Canterbury, 22
Uruguay Round, 87, 133
US Senate Foreign Relations Committee, 84
USS *Buchanan*, 112

van Bohemen, Gerard, *11*
Vance, Cyrus, 149–150
Vancouver, 118
Vanuatu, 114–115, 119–121
Vatican, 70
Venezuela, 151

Victoria University. *see* Te Herenga Waka
– Victoria University of Wellington
Viet Cong, 29, 32–34
Viet Minh, 32
Vietnam, 23, 25–26, 29–35, 55, 158
Vila, 115, 119–121
Villain, Claude, 96–97
Volunteer Service Abroad, 24

Walding, Joe, *2*, 36–40
Waldorf Astoria Hotel (New York), *12*,
141
Walter, Neil, 139
Washington, 18, 50, 82, 85, 101, 106,
128–130, 155, 160
Wat Mahatai, 22
Waterloo, 50, 60
Weir, Lady, 30
Weir, Sir Stephen, *15*, 22, 26, 29–32, 34
Wellington, 11–12, 17, 37–38, 40, 44,
83, 122, 146, 155, 158, 160, 162
early career in, 15, 19–20, 23–24
Western Sahara, 148
Wevers, Maarten, 77
whaling, 48–49
Whitehall, 45–46, 51
Wigram RAF base, 11
Wild Strawberries, 89
Wilde, Fran, *8*, 113, 124, 167
Wilford, Andrew, *16*

Willberg, Hilary, *11*
Wilson, Harold, 45, 48
Woluwe-Saint-Pierre, 110
Woodfield, Ted, *8*, 55, 86
Woods, Commodore, 124
World Bank, 24, 41, 85, 91
World Council of Churches, 83
World Court, 144
World Health Organization (WHO), 83,
85, 89
World Intellectual Property Organization
(WIPO), 83
World Meteorological Organization
(WMO), 83
World Trade Organization (WTO), 83,
87, 89, 143
World War I, 60, 109
World War II, 11, 26, 45, 56, 60, 65, 68,
109, 123, 141
World Wildlife Fund, 83
Wuhan, 39

Yangtze River, 39
Ypres, 109–110
Yugoslavia, 131, 149–150

Zeebrugge, 109
Zhou Enlai, *2*, 39
Zimbabwe, 140
Zurich, 90